Elizabeth Barrett Browning

Poems of the Intellect and the Affections

Elizabeth Barrett Browning

Poems of the Intellect and the Affections

ISBN/EAN: 9783743338708

Manufactured in Europe, USA, Canada, Australia, Japa

Cover: Foto ©ninafisch / pixelio.de

Manufactured and distributed by brebook publishing software (www.brebook.com)

Elizabeth Barrett Browning

Poems of the Intellect and the Affections

POEMS

OF THE

INTELLECT AND THE AFFECTIONS.

BY

ELIZABETH BARRETT BROWNING.

ELEGANTLY ILLUSTRATED.

PHILADELPHIA:
PUBLISHED BY E. H. BUTLER & CO.
1865.

ADVERTISEMENT.

To most persons who accost Mrs. Browning's Poems, for the first time, she presents a strange paradox. A woman, with such an individuality as seems to rise above the trammels of sex, she invades all the realms of thought, contests the palm of highest scholarship, and sings enthusiastic political songs in favor of regenerated Italy.

But Mrs. Browning is a true woman, after all. Her affections spring forth to greet the blinded Romney in Aurora Leigh, and her "Sonnets from the Portuguese," are as impassioned as any in the English language.

She has been accused of elliptical and confused diction. This is not just. Her works require an attentive reader, but once carefully studied they display a remarkably clear mind, subtle fancy, noble imagination, and the largest culture. In spite of ignorant critics, she has therefore gained a growing popularity, and is at present as extensively read in America as any other English poet.

Our careful selection has, as its aim, to render a truthful portraiture of her mind and heart, and thus to conduce to a more thorough knowledge of the greatest poet produced by England in our generation.

CONTENTS.

	PAGE
A Lament for Adonis	13
The Cry of the Children	18
The Lady's Yes	24
Heaven's Sunrise to Earth's Blindness	26
The Virgin Mary to the Child Jesus	27
From "Earth and her Praisers"	34
Crowned and Wedded	36
Crowned and Buried	39
False Step	46
Cowper's Grave	48
Hector in the Garden	51
Sleeping and Watching	55
The Seraph and Poet	57
Comfort	58
To George Sand	59
Heaven and Earth	59
A Song against Singing	60
Loved Once	62
A Child's Thought of God	64
The Sleep	65
The Weakest Thing	67
A Woman's Shortcomings	68

CONTENTS.

	PAGE
A Man's Requirements	70
Inclusions	72
Love for Love	72
A Lock of Hair	73
Call me by my Pet-Name	74
The Kiss	74
The Best Thing in the World	75
The Cry of the Human	76
My Kate	80
Amy's Cruelty	82
Garibaldi	84
Only a Curl	87
Mother and Poet	89
Napoleon III. in Italy	94
Christmas Gifts	110
A Curse for a Nation	112
Void in Law	117
May's Love	120
The Forced Recruit	120
King Victor Emanuel entering Florence, April, 1860	122

POEMS

OF

THE INTELLECT AND THE AFFECTIONS.

A LAMENT FOR ADONIS.

FROM BION.

I.

I MOURN for Adonis—Adonis is dead,
  Fair Adonis is dead and the Loves are lamenting.
Sleep, Cypris, no more on thy purple-strewed bed:
  Arise, wretch stoled in black; beat thy breast unrelenting,
And shriek to the worlds, "Fair Adonis is dead."

II.

I mourn for Adonis—the Loves are lamenting.
  He lies on the hills in his beauty and death;
The white tusk of a boar has transpierced his white thigh.
  Cytherea grows mad at his thin gasping breath,
While the black blood drips down on the pale ivory,
  And his eyeballs lie quenched with the weight of his brows.

CONTENTS.

	PAGE
A Man's Requirements	70
Inclusions	72
Love for Love	72
A Lock of Hair	73
Call me by my Pet-Name	74
The Kiss	74
The Best Thing in the World	75
The Cry of the Human	76
My Kate	80
Amy's Cruelty	82
Garibaldi	84
Only a Curl	87
Mother and Poet	89
Napoleon III. in Italy	94
Christmas Gifts	110
A Curse for a Nation	112
Void in Law	117
May's Love	120
The Forced Recruit	120
King Victor Emanuel entering Florence, April, 1860	122

POEMS

OF

THE INTELLECT AND THE AFFECTIONS.

A LAMENT FOR ADONIS.

FROM BION.

I.

I MOURN for Adonis—Adonis is dead,
    Fair Adonis is dead and the Loves are lamenting.
Sleep, Cypris, no more on thy purple-strewed bed:
    Arise, wretch stoled in black; beat thy breast unrelenting,
And shriek to the worlds, " Fair Adonis is dead."

II.

I mourn for Adonis—the Loves are lamenting.
    He lies on the hills in his beauty and death;
The white tusk of a boar has transpierced his white thigh.
    Cytherea grows mad at his thin gasping breath,
While the black blood drips down on the pale ivory,
    And his eyeballs lie quenched with the weight of his brows.

The rose fades from his lips, and upon them just parted
    The kiss dies the goddess consents not to lose,
Though the kiss of the Dead cannot make her glad-hearted:
    He knows not who kisses him dead in the dews.

III.

I mourn for Adonis—the Loves are lamenting.
    Deep, deep in the thigh is Adonis's wound,
But a deeper, is Cypris's bosom presenting.
    The youth lieth dead while his dogs howl around,
And the nymphs weep aloud from the mists of the hill,
    And the poor Aphrodité, with tresses unbound,
All dishevelled, unsandalled, shrieks mournful and shrill
    Through the dusk of the groves. The thorns, tearing her feet,
Gather up the red flower of her blood which is holy,
    Each footstep she takes; and the valleys repeat
The sharp cry she utters and draw it out slowly.
    She calls on her spouse, her Assyrian, on him
Her own youth, while the dark blood spreads over his body,
    The chest taking hue from the gash in the limb,
And the bosom once ivory, turning to ruddy.

IV.

Ah, ah, Cytherea! the Loves are lamenting.
    She lost her fair spouse and so lost her fair smile:
When he lived she was fair, by the whole world's consenting,
    Whose fairness is dead with him: woe worth the while!
All the mountains above and the oaklands below
    Murmur, ah, ah Adonis! the streams overflow

Aphrodité's deep wail; river-fountains in pity
  Weep soft in the hills, and the flowers as they blow
Redden outward with sorrow, while all hear her go
  With the song of her sadness through mountain and city.

v.

Ah, ah, Cytherea! Adonis is dead,
  Fair Adonis is dead—Echo answers, Adonis!
Who weeps not for Cypris, when bowing her head
  She stares at the wound where it gapes and astonies?
—When, ah, ah !—she saw how the blood ran away
  And empurpled the thigh, and, with wild hands flung out,
Said with sobs, "Stay, Adonis! unhappy one, stay,
  Let me feel thee once more, let me ring thee about
With the clasp of my arms, and press kiss into kiss!
  Wait a little, Adonis, and kiss me again,
For the last time, beloved,—and but so much of this
  That the kiss may learn life from the warmth of the strain!
—Till thy breath shall exude from thy soul to my mouth,
  To my heart, and, the love-charm I once more receiving,
May drink thy love in it and keep of a truth
  That one kiss in the place of Adonis the living.
Thou fliest me, mournful one, fliest me far,
  My Adonis, and seekest the Acheron portal,—
To Hell's cruel King goest down with a scar,
  While I weep and live on like a wretched immortal,
And follow no step! O Persephoné, take him,
  My husband!—thou'rt better and brighter than I.

So all beauty flows down to thee: *I* cannot make him
   Look up at my grief; there's despair in my cry,
Since I wail for Adonis who died to me—died to me—
     Then, I fear *thee!*—Art thou dead, my Adored?
Passion ends like a dream in the sleep that's denied to me.
   Cypris is widowed, the Loves seek their lord
All the house through in vain. Charm of cestus has ceased
   With thy clasp! O too bold in the hunt past preventing,
Ay, mad, thou so fair, to have strife with a beast!"
   Thus the goddess wailed on—and the Loves are lamenting.

VI.

Ah, ah, Cytherea! Adonis is dead.
   She wept tear after tear with the blood which was shed,
And both turned into flowers for the earth's garden-close,
   Her tears, to the wind-flower; his blood, to the rose.

VII.

I mourn for Adonis—Adonis is dead.
   Weep no more in the woods, Cytherea, thy lover!
So, well: make a place for his corse in thy bed,
   With the purples thou sleepest in, under and over.
He's fair though a corse—a fair corse, like a sleeper.
   Lay him soft in the silks he had pleasure to fold
When, beside thee at night, holy dreams deep and deeper
   Enclosed his young life on the couch made of gold.
Love him still, poor Adonis; cast on him together
   The crowns and the flowers: since he died from the place,

Why, let all die with him; let the blossoms go wither,
  Rain myrtles and olive-buds down on his face.
Rain the myrrh down, let all that is best fall a-pining,
  Since the myrrh of his life from thy keeping is swept.
Pale he lay, thine Adonis, in purples reclining;
  The Loves raised their voices around him and wept.
They have shorn their bright curls off to cast on Adonis;
One treads on his bow,—on his arrows, another,—
One breaks up a well-feathered quiver, and one is
  Bent low at a sandal, untying the strings,
And one carries the vases of gold from the springs,
While one washes the wound,—and behind them a brother
  Fans down on the body sweet air with his wings.

VIII.

Cytherea herself now the Loves are lamenting.
  Each torch at the door Hymenæus blew out;
And, the marriage-wreath dropping its leaves as repenting,
  No more "Hymen, Hymen," is chanted about,
But the *ai ai* instead—"ai alas" is begun
  For Adonis, and then follows "ai Hymenæus!"
The Graces are weeping for Cinyris' son,
  Sobbing low each to each, "His fair eyes cannot see us!"
Their wail strikes more shrill than the sadder Dioné's.
The Fates mourn aloud for Adonis, Adonis,
  Deep chanting; he hears not a word that they say:
  He *would* hear, but Persephoné has him in keeping.
—Cease moan, Cytherea: leave pomps for to-day,
  And weep new when a new year refits thee for weeping.

THE CRY OF THE CHILDREN.

I.

Do ye hear the children weeping, O my brothers,
    Ere the sorrow comes with years?
They are leaning their young heads against their mothers,
    And *that* cannot stop their tears.
The young lambs are bleating in the meadows,
    The young birds are chirping in the nest,
The young fawns are playing with the shadows,
    The young flowers are blowing toward the west—
But the young, young children, O my brothers,
    They are weeping bitterly!
They are weeping in the playtime of the others,
    In the country of the free.

II.

Do you question the young children in the sorrow
    Why their tears are falling so?
The old man may weep for his to-morrow
    Which is lost in Long Ago;
The old tree is leafless in the forest,
    The old year is ending in the frost,
The old wound, if stricken, is the sorest,
    The old hope is hardest to be lost:
But the young, young children, O my brothers,
    Do you ask them why they stand

Weeping sore before the bosoms of their mothers,
    In our happy Fatherland?

III.

They look up with their pale and sunken faces,
    And their looks are sad to see,
For the man's hoary anguish draws and presses
    Down the cheeks of infancy;
" Your old earth," they say, " is very dreary,
    Our young feet," they say, " are very weak;
Few paces have we taken, yet are weary—
    Our grave-rest is very far to seek:
Ask the aged why they weep, and not the children,
    For the outside earth is cold,
And we young ones stand without, in our bewildering,
    And the graves are for the old."

IV.

" True," say the children, " it may happen
    That we die before our time:
Little Alice died last year, her grave is shapen
    Like a snowball, in the rime.
We looked into the pit prepared to take her:
    Was no room for any work in the close clay!
From the sleep wherein she lieth none will wake her,
    Crying, " Get up, little Alice! it is day."
If you listen by that grave, in sun and shower,
    With your ear down, little Alice never cries;

Could we see her face, be sure we should not know her,
    For the smile has time for growing in her eyes:
And merry go her moments, lulled and stilled in
        The shroud by the kirk-chime.
It is good when it happens," say the children,
    " That we die before our time."

v.

Alas, alas, the children! they are seeking
    Death in life, as best to have:
They are binding up their hearts away from breaking,
    With a cerement from the grave.
Go out, children, from the mine and from the city,
    Sing out, children, as the little thrushes do;
Pluck your handfuls of the meadow-cowslips pretty,
    Laugh aloud, to feel your fingers let them through!
But they answer, " Are your cowslips of the meadows
    Like our weeds anear the mine?
Leave us quiet in the dark of the coal-shadows,
    From your pleasures fair and fine!

vi.

" For oh," say the children, " we are weary,
    And we cannot run or leap;
If we cared for any meadows, it were merely
    To drop down in them and sleep.
Our knees tremble sorely in the stooping,
    We fall upon our faces, trying to go;

And, underneath our heavy eyelids drooping,
  The reddest flower would look as pale as snow.
For, all day, we drag our burden tiring
    Through the coal-dark, underground;
Or, all day, we drive the wheels of iron
    In the factories, round and round.

VII.

" For all day, the wheels are droning, turning;
    Their wind comes in our faces,
Till our hearts turn, our heads with pulses burning,
    And the walls turn in their places:
Turns the sky in the high window blank and reeling,
    Turns the long light that drops adown the wall.
Turn the black flies that crawl along the ceiling,
    All are turning, all the day, and we with all.
And all day, the iron wheels are droning,
    And sometimes we could pray,
' O ye wheels,' (breaking out in a mad moaning)
    ' Stop! be silent for to-day!' "

VIII.

Ay, be silent! Let them hear each other breathing
    For a moment, mouth to mouth!
Let them touch each other's hands, in a fresh wreathing
    Of their tender human youth!
Let them feel that this cold metallic motion
    Is not all the life God fashions or reveals:

Let them prove their living souls against the notion
    That they live in you, or under you, O wheels!
Still, all day, the iron wheels go onward,
        Grinding life down from its mark;
And the children's souls, which God is calling sunward,
        Spin on blindly in the dark.

IX.

Now tell the poor young children, O my brothers,
    To look up to Him and pray;
So the blessed One who blesseth all the others,
    Will bless them another day.
They answer, "Who is God that he should hear us,
    While the rushing of the iron wheels is stirred?
When we sob aloud, the human creatures near us
    Pass by, hearing not, or answer not a word.
And *we* hear not (for the wheels in their resounding)
    Strangers speaking at the door:
Is it likely God, with angels singing round him,
    Hears our weeping any more?

X.

"Two words, indeed, of praying we remember,
    And at midnight's hour of harm,
'Our Father,' looking upward in the chamber,
    We say softly for a charm.
We know no other words except 'Our Father,'
    And we think that, in some pause of angels' song,

God may pluck them with the silence sweet to gather,
    And hold both within his right hand which is strong.
'Our Father!' If He heard us, He would surely
      (For they call him good and mild)
Answer, smiling down the steep world very purely,
    'Come and rest with me, my child.'

XI.

"But, no!" say the children, weeping faster,
    "He is speechless as a stone:
And they tell us, of his image is the master
    Who commands us to work on.
Go to!" say the children,—"up in Heaven,
    Dark, wheel-like, turning clouds are all we find.
Do not mock us; grief has made us unbelieving:
We look up for God, but tears have made us blind."
Do you hear the children weeping and disproving,
    O my brothers, what ye preach?
For God's possible is taught by His world's loving,
    And the children doubt of each.

XII.

And well may the children weep before you!
    They are weary ere they run;
They have never seen the sunshine, nor the glory
    Which is brighter than the sun.
They know the grief of man, without its wisdom;
    They sink in man's despair, without its calm;

Are slaves, without the liberty in Christdom,
　　Are martyrs, by the pang without the palm :
Are worn as if with age, yet unretrievingly
　　　　The harvest of its memories cannot reap,—
Are orphans of the earthly love and heavenly.
　　Let them weep! let them weep!

XIII.

They look up with their pale and sunken faces,
　　And their look is dread to see,
For they mind you of their angels in high places,
　　With eyes turned on Deity.
"How long," they say, "how long, O cruel nation,
　　Will you stand, to move the world, on a child's heart,—
Stifle down with a mailed heel its palpitation,
　　And tread onward to your throne amid the mart?
Our blood splashes upward, O gold-heaper,
　　And your purple shows your path !
But the child's sob in the silence curses deeper
　　Than the strong man in his wrath."

THE LADY'S YES.

"Yes," I answered you last night;
　　"No," this morning, sir, I say :
Colors seen by candle-light
　　Will not look the same by day.

THE LADY'S YES.

When the viols played their best,
    Lamps above and laughs below,
Love me sounded like a jest,
    Fit for *yes* or fit for *no*.

Call me false or call me free,
    Vow, whatever light may shine,—
No man on your face shall see
    Any grief for change on mine.

Yet the sin is on us both;
    Time to dance is not to woo;
Wooing light makes fickle troth,
    Scorn of *me* recoils on *you*.

Learn to win a lady's faith
    Nobly, as the thing is high,
Bravely, as for life and death,
    With a loyal gravity.

Lead her from the festive boards,
    Point her to the starry skies;
Guard her, by your truthful words,
    Pure from courtship's flatteries.

By your truth she shall be true,
    Ever true, as wives of yore;
And her *yes*, once said to you,
    SHALL be YES for evermore.

HEAVEN'S SUNRISE TO EARTH'S BLINDNESS.

       It is the hour for souls;
That bodies, leavened by the will and love,
Be lightened to redemption. The world's old;
But the old world waits the hour to be renewed:
Toward which, new hearts in individual growth
Must quicken, and increase to multitude
In new dynasties of the race of men,—
Developed whence, shall grow spontaneously
New churches, new œconomies, new laws
Admitting freedom, new societies
Excluding falsehood. He shall make all new.

  My Romney!—Lifting up my hand in his,
As wheeled by Seeing spirits toward the east,
He turned instinctively,—where, faint and fair,
Along the tingling desert of the sky,
Beyond the circle of the conscious hills,
Were laid in jasper-stone as clear as glass
The first foundations of that new, near Day
Which should be builded out of heaven, to God.
He stood a moment with erected brows,
In silence, as a creature might, who gazed:
Stood calm, and fed his blind, majestic eyes
Upon the thought of perfect noon. And when
I saw his soul saw,—"Jasper first," I said,

"And second, sapphire; third, chalcedony;
The rest in order, . . last, an amethyst."

THE VIRGIN MARY TO THE CHILD JESUS.

I.

Sleep, sleep, mine Holy One!
My flesh, my Lord!—what name? I do not know
A name that seemeth not too high or low,
    Too far from me or heaven:
My Jesus, *that* is best! that word being given
By the majestic angel whose command
Was softly as a man's beseeching said,
When I and all the earth appeared to stand
    In the great overflow
Of light celestial from his wings and head.
    Sleep, sleep, my saving One!

II.

And art Thou come for saving, baby-browed
And speechless Being—art Thou come for saving?
The palm that grows beside our door is bowed
By treadings of the low wind from the south,
A restless shadow through the chamber waving:
Upon its bough a bird sings in the sun,
But Thou, with that close slumber on Thy mouth,
Dost seem of wind and sun already weary.
Art come for saving, O my weary One?

III.

Perchance this sleep that shutteth out the dreary
Earth-sounds and motions, opens on Thy soul
      High dreams on fire with God;
High songs that make the pathways where they roll
More bright than stars do theirs; and visions new
Of Thine eternal Nature's old abode.
      Suffer this mother's kiss,
      Best thing that earthly is,
To glide the music and the glory through,
Nor narrow in thy dream the broad upliftings
      Of any seraph wing.
Thus noiseless, thus. Sleep, sleep, my dreaming One!

IV.

The slumber of his lips meseems to run
Through *my* lips to mine heart, to all its shiftings
Of sensual life, bringing contrariousness
In a great calm. I feel I could lie down
As Moses did, and die,*—and then live most.
I am 'ware of you, heavenly Presences,
That stand with your peculiar light unlost,
Each forehead with a high thought for a crown,
Unsunned i' the sunshine! I am 'ware. Ye throw
No shade against the wall! How motionless
Ye round me with your living statuary,

---

* It is a Jewish tradition that Moses died of the kisses of God's lips

THE VIRGIN MARY TO THE CHILD JESUS.

While through your whiteness, in and outwardly,
Continual thoughts of God appear to go,
Like light's soul in itself.   I bear, I bear
To look upon the dropt lids of your eyes,
Though their external shining testifies
To that beatitude within which were
Enough to blast an eagle at his sun :
I fall not on my sad clay face before ye,—
    I look on His.   I know
My spirit which dilateth with the woe
    Of His mortality,
    May well contain your glory.
    Yea, drop your lids more low.
Ye are but fellow-worshippers with me !
    Sleep, sleep, my worshipped One !

v.

We sate among the stalls at Bethlehem ;
The dumb kine from their fodder turning them,
    Softened their hornèd faces
    To almost human gazes
    Toward the newly Born :
The simple shepherds from the star-lit brooks
    Brought visionary looks,
As yet in their astonied hearing rung
    The strange sweet angel-tongue :
The magi of the East, in sandals worn,
    Knelt reverent, sweeping round,
  With long pale beards, their gifts upon the ground,

The incense, myrrh and gold
These baby-hands were impotent to hold:
So let all earthlies and celestials wait
    Upon Thy royal state.
  Sleep, sleep, my kingly One!

VI.

I am not proud—meek angels, ye invest
New meeknesses to hear such utterance rest
On mortal lips,—" I am not proud"—*not proud!*
Albeit in my flesh God sent His Son,
Albeit over Him my head is bowed
As others bow before Him, still mine heart
Bows lower than their knees. O centuries
That roll in vision your futurities
  My future grave athwart,—
Whose murmurs seem to reach me while I keep
  Watch o'er this sleep,—
Say of me as the Heavenly said—" Thou art
The blessedest of women!"—blessedest,
Not holiest, not noblest, no high name
Whose height misplaced may pierce me like a shame
When I sit meek in heaven!
              For me, for me,
God knows that I am feeble like the rest!
I often wandered forth, more child than maiden,
Among the midnight hills of Galilee,
  Whose summits looked heaven-laden,
Listening to silence as it seemed to be

God's voice, so soft yet strong, so fain to press
Upon my heart as heaven did on the height,
And waken up its shadows by a light,
And show its vileness by a holiness.
Then I knelt down most silent like the night.
  Too self-renounced for fears,
Raising my small face to the boundless blue
Whose stars did mix and tremble in my tears:
God heard *them* falling after, with his dew.

VII.

So, seeing my corruption, can I see
This Incorruptible now born of me,
This fair new Innocence no sun did chance
To shine on, (for even Adam was no child)
Created from my nature all defiled,
This mystery, from out mine ignorance,—
Nor feel the blindness, stain, corruption, more
Than others do, or *I* did heretofore?
Can hands wherein such burden pure has been,
Not open with the cry, " unclean, unclean,"
More oft than any else beneath the skies?
  Ah King, ah Christ, ah son!
The kine, the shepherds, the abasèd wise
  Must all less lowly wait
  Than I, upon Thy state.
 Sleep, sleep, my kingly One!

VIII.

Art Thou a King, then?   Come, His universe,
   Come, crown me Him a King!
Pluck rays from all such stars as never fling
   Their light where fell a curse,
And make a crowning for this kingly brow!—
What is my word?   Each empyreal star
      Sits in a sphere afar
      In shining ambuscade:
      The child-brow, crowned by none,
      Keeps its unchildlike shade.
      Sleep, sleep, my crownless One!

IX.

Unchildlike shade!   No other babe doth wear
An aspect very sorrowful, as Thou.
No small babe-smiles my watching heart has seen
To float like speech the speechless lips between,
No dovelike cooing in the golden air,
No quick short joys of leaping babyhood:
      Alas, our earthly good
In heaven thought evil, seems too good for Thee:
      Yet, sleep, my weary One!

X.

And then the drear sharp tongue of prophecy,
With the dread sense of things which shall be done,
Doth smite me inly, like a sword: a sword?

That "smites the Shepherd." Then, I think aloud
The words " despised,"—" rejected,"—every word
Recoiling into darkness as I view
    The DARLING on my knee.
Bright angels,—move not—lest ye stir the cloud
Betwixt my soul and His futurity!
I must not die, with mother's work to do,
    And could not live—and see.

XI.

    It is enough to bear
    This image still and fair,
    This holier in sleep
    Than a saint at prayer,
    This aspect of a child
    Who never sinned or smiled;
This Presence in an infant's face;
This sadness most like love,
This love than love more deep,
This weakness like omnipotence
It is so strong to move.
Awful is this watching place,
Awful what I see from hence—
A king, without regalia,
A God, without the thunder,
A child, without the heart for play;
Ay, a Creator, rent asunder
From His first glory and cast away

On His own world, for me alone
To hold in hands created, crying—Son!

XII.

That tear fell not on Thee,
Beloved, yet thou stirrest in thy slumber!
Thou, stirring not for glad sounds out of number
Which through the vibratory palm-trees run
 From summer-wind and bird,
 So quickly hast thou heard
 A tear fall silently?
 Wak'st thou, O loving One?—

FROM "EARTH AND HER PRAISERS."

Praised be the mosses soft
In thy forest pathways oft,
And the thorns, which make us think
Of the thornless river-brink
 Where the ransomed tread:
Praisèd be thy sunny gleams,
And the storm, that worketh dreams
 Of calm unfinished:
Praisèd be thine active days,
And thy night-time's solemn need,
When in God's dear book we read
 No night shall be therein:

Praisèd be thy dwellings warm
By household faggot's cheerful blaze,
Where, to hear of pardoned sin,
Pauseth oft the merry din,
Save the babe's upon the arm
Who croweth to the crackling wood:
Yea, and, better understood,
Praisèd be thy dwellings cold,
Hid beneath the churchyard mould,
Where the bodies of the saints
Separate from earthly taints
Lie asleep, in blessing bound,
Waiting for the trumpet's sound
To free them into blessing;—none
Weeping more beneath the sun,
Though dangerous words of human love
Be graven very near, above.

Earth, we Christians praise thee thus,
Even for the change that comes
With a grief from thee to us:
For thy cradles and thy tombs,
For the pleasant corn and wine
And summer-heat; and also for
The frost upon the sycamore
    And hail upon the vine!

CROWNED AND WEDDED.

I.

WHEN last before her people's face her own fair face she bent,
Within the meek projection of that shade she was content
To erase the child-smile from her lips, which seemed as if it might
Be still kept holy from the world to childhood still in sight—
To erase it with a solemn vow, a princely vow—to rule,
A priestly vow—to rule by grace of God the pitiful,
A very godlike vow—to rule in right and righteousness
And with the law and for the land—so God the vower bless!

II.

The minster was alight that day, but not with fire, I ween,
And long-drawn glitterings swept adown that mighty aislèd scene;
The priests stood stolèd in their pomp, the sworded chiefs in theirs,
And so, the collared knights, and so, the civil ministers,
And so, the waiting lords and dames, and little pages best
At holding trains, and legates so, from countries east and west;
So, alien princes, native peers, and high-born ladies bright,
Along whose brows the Queen's, now crowned, flashed coronets to light;
And so, the people at the gates with priestly hands on high
Which bring the first anointing to all legal majesty;
And so the DEAD, who lie in rows beneath the minster floor,
There verily an awful state maintaining evermore;
The statesman whose clean palm will kiss no bribe whate'er it be,
The courtier who for no fair queen will rise up to his knee,

The court-dame who for no court-tire will leave her shroud behind,
The laureate who no courtlier rhyme than "dust to dust" can find,
The kings and queens who having made that vow and worn that crown,
Descended unto lower thrones and darker, deep adown:
Dieu et mon droit—what is't to them? what meaning can it have?—
The King of kings, the right of death—God's judgment and the grave.
And when betwixt the quick and dead the young fair queen had vowed,
The living shouted, "May she live! Victoria, live!" aloud:
And as the loyal shouts went up, true spirits prayed between,
"The blessings happy monarchs have be thine, O crownèd queen!"

III.

But now before her people's face she bendeth hers anew,
And calls them, while she vows, to be her witness thereunto.
She vowed to rule, and in that oath her childhood put away:
She doth maintain her womanhood, in vowing love to-day.
O lovely lady! let her vow! such lips become such vows,
And fairer goeth bridal wreath than crown with vernal brows.
O lovely lady! let her vow! yea, let her vow to love!
And though she be no less a queen, with purples hung above,
The pageant of a court behind, the royal kin around,
And woven gold to catch her looks turned maidenly to ground,
Yet may the bride-veil hide from her a little of that state,
While loving hopes for retinues about her sweetness wait.

She vows to love who vowed to rule—(the chosen at her side)
Let none say, God preserve the queen! but rather, Bless the
    bride!
None blow the trump, none bend the knee, none violate the dream
Wherein no monarch but a wife she to herself may seem.
Or if ye say, Preserve the queen! oh, breathe it inward low—
She is a *woman*, and *beloved!* and 'tis enough but so.
Count it enough, thou noble prince who tak'st her by the hand
And claimest for thy lady-love our lady of the land!
And since, Prince Albert, men have called thy spirit high and
    rare,
And true to truth and brave for truth as some at Augsburg were,
We charge thee by thy lofty thoughts and by thy poet-mind
Which not by glory and degree takes measure of mankind,
Esteem that wedded hand less dear for sceptre than for ring,
And hold her uncrowned womanhood to be the royal thing.

IV.

And now, upon our queen's last vow what blessings shall we pray?
None straitened to a shallow crown will suit our lips to-day:
Behold, they must be free as love, they must be broad as free,
Even to the borders of heaven's light and earth's humanity.
Long live she!—send up loyal shouts, and true hearts pray
    between,—
"The blessings happy PEASANTS have, be thine, O crownèd
    queen!"

CROWNED AND BURIED.

I.

Napoleon!—years ago, and that great word
Compact of human breath in hate and dread
And exultation, skied us overhead—
An atmosphere whose lightning was the sword
Scathing the cedars of the world,—drawn down
In burnings, by the metal of a crown.

II.

Napoleon!—nations, while they cursed that name,
Shook at their own curse; and while others bore
Its sound, as of a trumpet, on before,
Brass-fronted legions justified its fame;
And dying men on trampled battle-sods
Near their last silence uttered it for God's.

III.

Napoleon!—sages, with high foreheads drooped,
Did use it for a problem; children small
Leapt up to greet it, as at manhood's call;
Priests blessed it from their altars overstooped
By meek-eyed Christs; and widows with a moan
Spake it, when questioned why they sate alone.

IV.

That name consumed the silence of the snows
In Alpine keeping, holy and cloud-hid;

The mimic eagles dared what Nature's did,
And over-rushed her mountainous repose
In search of eyries: and the Egyptian river
Mingled the same word with its grand " For ever."

v.

That name was shouted near the pyramidal
Nilotic tombs, whose mummied habitants,
Packed to humanity's significance,
Motioned it back with stillness,—shouts as idle
As hireling artists' work of myrrh and spice
Which swathed last glories round the Ptolemies.

vi.

The world's face changed to hear it; kingly men
Came down in chidden babes' bewilderment
From autocratic places, each content
With sprinkled ashes for anointing: then
The people laughed or wondered for the nonce,
To see one throne a composite of thrones.

vii.

Napoleon!—even the torrid vastitude
Of India felt in throbbings of the air
That name which scattered by disastrous blare
All Europe's bound-lines,—drawn afresh in blood.
Napoleon!—from the Russias west to Spain:
And Austria trembled till ye heard her chain.

VIII.

And Germany was 'ware; and Italy
Oblivious of old fames—her laurel-locked,
High-ghosted Cæsars passing uninvoked—
Did crumble her own ruins with her knee,
To serve a newer: ay! but Frenchmen cast
A future from them nobler than her past:

IX.

For verily though France augustly rose
With that raised NAME, and did assume by such
The purple of the world, none gave so much
As she in purchase—to speak plain, in loss—
Whose hands, toward freedom stretched, dropped paralyzed
To wield a sword or fit an undersized

X.

King's crown to a great man's head. And though along
Her Paris' streets, did float on frequent streams
Of triumph, pictured or enmarbled dreams
Dreamt right by genius in a world gone wrong,—
No dream of all so won was fair to see
As the lost vision of her liberty.

XI.

Napoleon!—'twas a high name lifted high:
It met at last God's thunder sent to clear
Our compassing and covering atmosphere

And open a clear sight beyond the sky
Of supreme empire; this of earth's was done—
And kings crept out again to feel the sun.

XII.

The kings crept out—the peoples sate at home,
And finding the long-invocated peace
(A pall embroidered with worn images
Of rights divine) too scant to cover doom
Such as they suffered, cursed the corn that grew
Rankly, to bitter bread, on Waterloo.

XIII.

A deep gloom centered in the deep repose;
The nations stood up mute to count their dead:
And he who owned the NAME which vibrated
Through silence,—trusting to his noblest foes
When earth was all too gray for chivalry,
Died of their mercies 'mid the desert sea.

XIV.

O wild St. Helen! very still she kept him,
With a green willow for all pyramid,
Which stirred a little if the low wind did.
A little more, if pilgrims overwept him,
Disparting the lithe boughs to see the clay
Which seemed to cover his for judgment-day.

XV.

Nay, not so long! France kept her old affection
As deeply as the sepulchre the corse;

Until, dilated by such love's remorse
To a new angel of the resurrection,
She cried, "Behold, thou England! I would have
The dead whereof thou wottest, from that grave."

XVI.

And England answered in the courtesy
Which, ancient foes turned lovers, may befit,—
"Take back thy dead! and when thou buriest it,
Throw in all former strifes 'twixt thee and me."
Amen, mine England! 'tis a courteous claim:
But ask a little room too—for thy shame!

XVII.

Because it was not well, it was not well,
Nor tuneful with thy lofty-chanted part
Among the Oceanides,—that Heart
To bind and bare and vex with vulture fell.
I would, my noble England, men might seek
All crimson stains upon thy breast—not cheek!

XVIII.

I would that hostile fleets had scarred Torbay,
Instead of the lone ship which waited moored
Until thy princely purpose was assured,
Then left a shadow, not to pass away—
Not for to-night's moon, nor to-morrow's sun:
Green watching hills, ye witnessed what was done!*

* Written at Torquay.

XIX.

But since it *was* done,—in sepulchral dust
We fain would pay back something of our debt
To France, if not to honor, and forget
How through much fear we falsified the trust
Of a fallen foe and exile. We return
Orestes to Electra—in his urn.

XX.

A little urn—a little dust inside,
Which once outbalanced the large earth, albeit
To-day a four-years child might carry it
Sleek-browed and smiling, "Let the burden 'bide!"
Orestes to Electra!—O fair town
Of Paris, how the wild tears will run down

XXI.

And run back in the chariot-marks of time.
When all the people shall come forth to meet
The passive victor, death-still in the street
He rode through 'mid the shouting and bell-chime
And martial music, under eagles which
Dyed their rapacious beaks at Austerlitz!

XXII.

Napoleon!—he hath come again, borne home
Upon the popular ebbing heart,—a sea
Which gathers its own wrecks perpetually,
Majestically moaning. Give him room!

Room for the dead in Paris! welcome solemn
And grave-deep, 'neath the cannon-moulded column!*

XXIII.

There, weapon spent and warrior spent may rest
From roar of fields,—provided Jupiter
Dare trust Saturnus to lie down so near
His bolts!—and this he may: for, dispossessed
Of any godship lies the godlike arm—
The goat, Jove sucked, as likely to do harm.

XXIV.

And yet . . . Napoleon!—the recovered name
Shakes the old casements of the world; and we
Look out upon the passing pageantry,
Attesting that the Dead makes good his claim
To a French grave,—another kingdom won,
The last, of few spans—by Napoleon.

XXV.

Blood fell like dew beneath his sunrise—sooth!
But glittered dew-like in the covenanted
Meridian light. He was a despot—granted!
But the αυτος of his autocratic mouth
Said yea i' the people's French; he magnified
The image of the freedom he denied:

---

* It was the first intention to bury him under the column.

XXVI.

And if they asked for rights, he made reply
" Ye have my glory!"—and so, drawing round them
His ample purple, glorified and bound them
In an embrace that seemed identity.
He ruled them like a tyrant—true! but none
Were ruled like slaves: each felt Napoleon.

XXVII.

I do not praise this man: the man was flawed
For Adam—much more, Christ!—his knee unbent,
His hand unclean, his aspiration pent
Within a sword-sweep—pshaw!—but since he had
The genius to be loved, why let him have
The justice to be honored in his grave.

XXVIII.

I think this nation's tears thus poured together,
Better than shouts. I think this funeral
Grander than crownings, though a Pope bless all.
I think this grave stronger than thrones. But whether
The crowned Napoleon or the buried clay
Be worthier, I discern not: angels may.

FALSE STEP.

Sweet, thou hast trod on a heart.
   Pass! there's a world full of men;

And women as fair as thou art
    Must do such things now and then.

Thou only hast stepped unaware,—
    Malice, not one can impute;
And why should a heart have been there
    In the way of a fair woman's foot?

It was not a stone that could trip,
    Nor was it a thorn that could rend:
Put up thy proud underlip!
    'Twas merely the heart of a friend.

And yet peradventure one day
    Thou, sitting alone at the glass,
Remarking the bloom gone away,
    Where the smile in its dimplement was,

And seeking around thee in vain
    From hundreds who flattered before,
Such a word as, "Oh, not in the main
    Do I hold thee less precious, but more!"

Thou'lt sigh, very like, on thy part,
    "Of all I have known or can know,
I wish I had only that Heart
    I trod upon ages ago!"

COWPER'S GRAVE.

It is a place where poets crowned may feel the heart's decaying;
It is a place where happy saints may weep amid their praying:
Yet let the grief and humbleness as low as silence languish:
Earth surely now may give her calm to whom she gave her anguish.

O poets, from a maniac's tongue was poured the deathless singing!
O Christians, at your cross of hope a hopeless hand was clinging!
O men, this man in brotherhood your weary paths beguiling,
Groaned inly while he taught you peace, and died while ye were smiling!

And now, what time ye all may read through dimming tears his story,
How discord on the music fell and darkness on the glory,
And how when, one by one, sweet sounds and wandering lights departed,
He wore no less a loving face because so broken-hearted,

He shall be strong to sanctify the poet's high vocation,
And bow the meekest Christian down in meeker adoration;
Nor ever shall he be, in praise, by wise or good forsaken,
Named softly as the household name of one whom God hath taken.

With quiet sadness and no gloom I learn to think upon him,
With meekness that is gratefulness to God whose heaven hath won him,

Who suffered once the madness-cloud to His own love to blind him,
But gently led the blind along where breath and bird could find him;

And wrought within his shattered brain such quick poetic senses
As hills have language for, and stars, harmonious influences:
The pulse of dew upon the grass kept his within its number.
And silent shadows from the trees refreshed him like a slumber.

Wild timid hares were drawn from woods to share his home-caresses,
Uplooking to his human eyes with sylvan tendernesses:
The very world, by God's constraint, from falsehood's ways removing,
Its women and its men became, beside him, true and loving.

And though, in blindness, he remained unconscious of that guiding,
And things provided came without the sweet sense of providing.
He testified this solemn truth, while phrenzy desolated,
—Nor man nor nature satisfies whom only God created.

Like a sick child that knoweth not his mother while she blesses
And drops upon his burning brow the coolness of her kisses,—
That turns his fevered eyes around—" My mother! where's my mother?"—
As if such tender words and deeds could come from any other!—

The fever gone, with leaps of heart he sees her bending o'er him,
Her face all pale from watchful love, the unweary love she bore him!—
Thus woke the poet from the dream his life's long fever gave him,
Beneath those deep pathetic Eyes which closed in death to save him.

Thus? oh, not *thus!* no type of earth can image that awaking,
Wherein he scarcely heard the chant of seraphs, round him breaking,
Or felt the new immortal throb of soul from body parted,
But felt those eyes alone, and knew,—" *My Saviour! not* deserted!"

Deserted! Who hath dreamt that when the cross in darkness rested,
Upon the Victim's hidden face no love was manifested?
What frantic hands outstretched have e'er the atoning drops averted?
What tears have washed them from the soul, that *one* should be deserted?

Deserted! God could separate from His own essence rather;
And Adam's sins *have* swept between the righteous Son and Father:
Yea, once, Immanuel's orphaned cry His universe hath shaken—
It went up single, echoless, " My God, I am forsaken!"

It went up from the Holy's lips amid His lost creation,
That, of the lost, no son should use those words of desolation!
That earth's worst phrenzies, marring hope, should mar not
    hope's fruition,
And I, on Cowper's grave, should see his rapture in a vision.

HECTOR IN THE GARDEN.

NINE years old! The first of any
    Seem the happiest years that come:
    Yet when *I* was nine, I said
    No such word! I thought instead
That the Greeks had used as many
    In besieging Ilium.

Nine green years had scarcely brought me
    To my childhood's haunted spring;
    I had life, like flowers and bees
    In betwixt the country trees,
And the sun the pleasure taught me
    Which he teacheth everything.

If the rain fell, there was sorrow,
    Little head leant on the pane,
    Little finger drawing down it
    The long trailing drops upon it,
And the "Rain, rain, come to-morrow,"
    Said for charm against the rain.

Such a charm was right Canidian
  Though you meet it with a jeer!
  If I said it long enough,
  Then the rain hummed dimly off
And the thrush with his pure Lydian
  Was left only to the ear;

And the sun and I together
  Went a-rushing out of doors:
  We our tender spirits drew
  Over hill and dale in view,
Glimmering hither, glimmering thither,
  In the footsteps of the showers.

Underneath the chestnuts dripping,
  Through the grasses wet and fair,
  Straight I sought my garden-ground
  With the laurel on the mound,
And the pear-tree oversweeping
  A side-shadow of green air.

In the garden lay supinely
  A huge giant wrought of spade!
  Arms and legs were stretched at length
  In a passive giant strength,—
The fine meadow-turf, cut finely,
  Round them laid and interlaid.

Call him Hector, son of Priam!
  Such his title and degree.

With my rake I smoothed his brow,
    Both his cheeks I weeded through,
But a rhymer such as I am,
    Scarce can sing his dignity.

Eyes of gentianellas azure,
    Staring, winking at the skies;
    Nose of gillyflowers and box;
    Scented grasses put for locks,
Which a little breeze at pleasure
    Set a-waving round his eyes:

Brazen helm of daffodillies,
    With a glitter toward the light;
    Purple violets for the mouth,
    Breathing perfumes west and south;
And a sword of flashing lilies,
    Holden ready for the fight:

And a breastplate made of daisies,
    Closely fitting, leaf on leaf;
    Periwinkles interlaced
    Drawn for belt about the waist;
While the brown bees, humming praises,
    Shot their arrows round the chief.

And who knows, (I sometimes wondered,)
    If the disembodied soul
    Of old Hector, once of Troy,
    Might not take a dreary joy

Here to enter—if it thundered,
   Rolling up the thunder-roll?

Rolling this way from Troy-ruin,
   In this body rude and rife
   Just to enter, and take rest
   'Neath the daisies of the breast—
They, with tender roots, renewing
   His heroic heart to life?

Who could know? I sometimes started
   At a motion or a sound!
   Did his mouth speak—naming Troy
   With an ototototoi?
Did the pulse of the Strong-hearted
   Make the daisies tremble round?

It was hard to answer, often:
   But the birds sang in the tree,
   But the little birds sang bold
   In the pear-tree green and old,
And my terror seemed to soften
   Through the courage of their glee.

Oh, the birds, the tree, the ruddy
   And white blossoms sleek with rain!
   Oh, my garden rich with pansies!
   Oh, my childhood's bright romances!
All revive, like Hector's body,
   And I see them stir again.

And despite life's changes, chances,
   And despite the deathbell's toll,
They press on me in full seeming:
   Help, some angel! stay this dreaming!
As the birds sang in the branches,
   Sing God's patience through my soul!

That no dreamer, no neglecter
   Of the present's work unsped,
I may wake up and be doing,
   Life's heroic ends pursuing,
Though my past is dead as Hector,
   And though Hector is twice dead.

SLEEPING AND WATCHING.

I.

Sleep on, baby, on the floor,
   Tired of all the playing:
Sleep with smile the sweeter for
   That, you dropped away in.
On your curls' full roundness stand
   Golden lights serenely;
One cheek, pushed out by the hand,
   Folds the dimple inly:
Little head and little foot
   Heavy laid for pleasure,

Underneath the lids half shut,
   Slants the shining azure.
Open-soul in noon-day sun,
   So you lie and slumber:
Nothing evil having done,
   Nothing can encumber.

II.

I, who cannot sleep as well,
   Shall I sigh to view you?
Or sigh further to foretell
   All that may undo you?
Nay, keep smiling, little child,
   Ere the sorrow neareth:
I will smile too! patience mild
   Pleasure's token weareth.
Nay, keep sleeping before loss:
   I shall sleep though losing!
As by cradle, so by cross,
   Sure is the reposing.

III.

And God knows who sees us twain,
   Child at childish leisure,
I am near as tired of pain
   As you seem of pleasure.
Very soon too, by His grace
   Gently wrapt around me,

THE SERAPH AND POET.

Shall I show as calm a face,
   Shall I sleep as soundly.
Differing in this, that you
   Clasp your playthings, sleeping,
While my hands shall drop the few
   Given to my keeping:
Differing in this, that I
   Sleeping shall be colder,
And in waking presently,
   Brighter to beholder:
Differing in this beside
   (Sleeper, have you heard me?
Do you move, and open wide
   Eyes of wonder toward me?)—
That while you I thus recall
   From your sleep, I solely,
Me from mine an angel shall,
   With reveillie holy.

THE SERAPH AND POET.

THE seraph sings before the manifest
God-One, and in the burning of the Seven,
And with the full life of consummate Heaven
Heaving beneath him like a mother's breast
Warm with her first-born's slumber in that nest.

The poet sings upon the earth grave-riven,
Before the naughty world, soon self-forgiven
For wronging him,—and in the darkness pressed
From his own soul by worldly weights. Even so,
Sing, seraph with the glory! heaven is high;
Sing, poet with the sorrow! earth is low:
The universe's inward voices cry
" Amen" to either song of joy and woe:
Sing, seraph,—poet,—sing on equally!

COMFORT.

Speak low to me, my Saviour, low and sweet
From out the hallelujahs, sweet and low,
Lest I should fear and fall, and miss Thee so
Who art not missed by any that entreat.
Speak to me as to Mary at Thy feet!
And if no precious gums my hands bestow,
Let my tears drop like amber while I go
In reach of Thy divinest voice complete
In humanest affection—thus, in sooth,
To lose the sense of losing. As a child,
Whose song-bird seeks the wood for evermore,
Is sung to in its stead by mother's mouth
Till, sinking on her breast, love-reconciled,
He sleeps the faster that he wept before.

TO GEORGE SAND.

A RECOGNITION.

TRUE genius, but true woman! dost deny
The woman's nature with a manly scorn,
And break away the gauds and armlets worn
By weaker women in captivity?
Ah, vain denial! that revolted cry
Is sobbed in by a woman's voice forlorn,—
Thy woman's hair, my sister, all unshorn
Floats back dishevelled strength in agony,
Disproving thy man's name: and while before
The world thou burnest in a poet-fire,
We see thy woman-heart beat evermore
Through the large flame. Beat purer, heart, and higher,
Till God unsex thee on the heavenly shore
Where unincarnate spirits purely aspire!

HEAVEN AND EARTH.

"And there was silence in heaven for the space of half an hour."
Revelation.

GOD, who with thunders and great voices kept
Beneath Thy throne, and stars most silver-paced
Along the inferior gyres, and open-faced
Melodious angels round,—canst intercept
Music with music,—yet, at will, hast swept

All back, all back, (said he in Patmos placed)
To fill the heavens with silence of the waste
Which lasted half an hour!—lo, I who have wept
All day and night, beseech Thee by my tears,
And by that dread response of curse and groan
Men alternate across these hemispheres,
Vouchsafe us such a half-hour's hush alone,
In compensation for our stormy years:
As heaven has paused from song, let earth from moan!

A SONG AGAINST SINGING.

They bid me sing to thee,
Thou golden-haired and silver-voicèd child—
With lips by no worse sigh than sleep's defiled—
With eyes unknowing how tears dim the sight,
And feet all trembling at the new delight
    Treaders of earth to be!

Ah no! the lark may bring
A song to thee from out the morning cloud,
The merry river from its lilies bowed,
The brisk rain from the trees, the lucky wind
That half doth make its music, half doth find,—
    But *I*—I may not sing.

A SONG AGAINST SINGING.

  How could I think it right,
New-comer on our earth as, Sweet, thou art,
To bring a verse from out an human heart
Made heavy with accumulated tears,
And cross with such amount of weary years
  Thy day-sum of delight?

  Even if the verse were said,
Thou, who wouldst clap thy tiny hands to hear
The wind or rain, gay bird or river clear,
Wouldst, at that sound of sad humanities,
Upturn thy bright uncomprehending eyes
  And bid me play instead.

  Therefore no song of mine,—
But prayer in place of singing; prayer that would
Commend thee to the new-creating God
Whose gift is childhood's heart without its stain
Of weakness, ignorance, and changing vain—
  That gift of God be thine!

  So wilt thou aye be young,
In lovelier childhood than thy shining brow
And pretty winning accents make thee now:
Yea, sweeter than this scarce articulate sound
(How sweet!) of "father," "mother," shall be found
  The ABBA on thy tongue.

  And so, as years shall chase
Each other's shadows, thou wilt less resemble

Thy fellows of the earth who toil and tremble,
Than him thou seest not, thine angel bold
Yet meek, whose ever-lifted eyes behold
    The Ever-loving's face.

LOVED ONCE.

I CLASSED, appraising once,
Earth's lamentable sounds,—the welladay,
    The jarring yea and nay,
The fall of kisses on unanswering clay,
The sobbed farewell, the welcome mournfuller,—
    But all did leaven the air
With a less bitter leaven of sure despair
    Than these words—" I loved ONCE."

And who saith, " I loved ONCE"?
Not angels,—whose clear eyes, love, love foresee,
    Love, through eternity,
And by To Love do apprehend To Be.
Not God, called LOVE, His noble crown-name casting
    A light too broad for blasting:
The great God changing not from everlasting,
    Saith never, " I loved ONCE."

Oh, never is " Loved ONCE"
Thy word, thou Victim-Christ, misprizèd friend!
    Thy cross and curse may rend,

But having loved Thou lovest to the end.
This is man's saying—man's: too weak to move
    One spherèd star above.
Man desecrates the eternal God-word Love
    By his No More, and Once.

How say ye, " We loved once,"
Blasphemers ? Is your earth not cold enow.
    Mourners, without that snow ?
Ah, friends, and would ye wrong each other so ?
And could ye say of some whose love is known,
    Whose prayers have met your own,
Whose tears have fallen for you, whose smiles have shone
    So long,—" We loved them ONCE" ?

Could ye, " We loved her once,"
Say calm of me, sweet friends, when out of sight ?
    When hearts of better right
Stand in between me and your happy light ?
Or when, as flowers kept too long in the shade,
    Ye find my colors fade.
And all that is not love in me, decayed ?
    Such words—Ye loved me ONCE !

Could ye, " We loved her ONCE"
Say cold of me when further put away
    In earth's sepulchral clay,
When mute the lips which deprecate to-day ?
Not so ! not then—least then ! When life is shriven
    And death's full joy is given,—

Of those who sit and love you up in heaven,
    Say not, "We loved them once."

Say never, ye loved ONCE:
God is too near above, the grave, beneath,
    And all our moments breathe
Too quick in mysteries of life and death,
For such a word. The eternities avenge
    Affections light of range.
There comes no change to justify that change.
    Whatever comes—Loved ONCE!

And yet that same word ONCE
Is humanly acceptive. Kings have said
    Shaking a discrowned head,
"We ruled once,"—dotards, "We once taught and led."
Cripples once danced i' the vines, and bards approved,
    Were once by scornings moved:
But love strikes one hour—LOVE! those *never* loved
    Who dream that they loved ONCE.

A CHILD'S THOUGHT OF GOD.

They say that God lives very high;
    But if you look above the pines
You cannot see our God; and why?

And if you dig down in the mines
    You never see Him in the gold;
Though from Him all that's glory shines.

God is so good, He wears a fold
    Of heaven and earth across His face—
Like secrets kept, for love, untold.

But still I feel that His embrace
    Slides down by thrills, through all things made,
Through sight and sound of every place.

As if my tender mother laid
    On my shut lips her kisses' pressure,
Half-waking me at night, and said
    "Who kissed you through the dark, dear guesser?"

THE SLEEP.

"He giveth His beloved sleep."—*Psalm* cxxvii. 2.

Of all the thoughts of God that are
Borne inward into souls afar,
Along the Psalmist's music deep,
Now tell me if that any is,
For gift or grace, surpassing this—
"He giveth His belovèd, sleep"?

What would we give to our beloved?
The hero's heart to be unmoved,
The poet's star-tuned harp to sweep,
The patriot's voice to teach and rouse,
The monarch's crown to light the brows?—
He giveth His belovèd, sleep.

What do we give to our beloved?
A little faith all undisproved,
A little dust to overweep,
And bitter memories to make
The whole earth blasted for our sake:
He giveth His belovèd, sleep.

"Sleep soft, beloved!" we sometimes say,
Who have no tune to charm away
Sad dreams that through the eyelids creep:
But never doleful dream again
Shall break the happy slumber when
He giveth His belovèd, sleep.

O earth, so full of dreary noises!
O men, with wailing in your voices!
O delvèd gold, the wailers heap!
O strife, O curse, that o'er it fall!
God strikes a silence through you all,
And giveth His belovèd, sleep.

His dews drop mutely on the hill,
His cloud above it saileth still,
Though on its slope men sow and reap:
More softly than the dew is shed,
Or cloud is floated overhead,
He giveth His belovèd, sleep.

Ay, men may wonder while they scan
A living, thinking, feeling man

Confirmed in such a rest to keep;
But angels say, and through the word
I think their happy smile is *heard*—
"He giveth His belovèd, sleep."

For me, my heart that erst did go
Most like a tired child at a show,
That sees through tears the mummers leap,
Would now its wearied vision close,
Would childlike on His love repose
Who giveth His belovèd, sleep.

And friends, dear friends, when it shall be
That this low breath is gone from me,
And round my bier ye come to weep,
Let One, most loving of you all,
Say, "Not a tear must o'er her fall!
He giveth His belovèd, sleep."

THE WEAKEST THING.

WHICH is the weakest thing of all
    Mine heart can ponder?
The sun, a little cloud can pall
    With darkness yonder?
The cloud, a little wind can move
    Where'er it listeth?
The wind, a little leaf above,
    Though sere, resisteth?

What time that yellow leaf was green,
  My days were gladder;
But now, whatever Spring may mean,
  I must grow sadder.
Ah me! a *leaf* with sighs can wring
  My lips asunder?
Then is mine heart the weakest thing
  Itself can ponder.

Yet, Heart, when sun and cloud are pined
  And drop together,
And at a blast which is not wind,
  The forests wither,
Thou, from the darkening deathly curse,
  To glory breakest,—
The strongest of the universe
  Guarding the weakest!

A WOMAN'S SHORTCOMINGS.

She has laughed as softly as if she sighed.
  She has counted six, and over,
Of a purse well filled, and a heart well tried—
  Oh, each a worthy lover!
They "give her time;" for her soul must slip
  Where the world has set the grooving:
She will lie to none with her fair red lip—
  But love seeks truer loving.

A WOMAN'S SHORTCOMINGS.

She trembles her fan in a sweetness dumb,
   As her thoughts were beyond recalling,
With a glance for *one*, and a glance for *some*,
   From her eyelids rising and falling;
Speaks common words with a blushful air,
   Hears bold words, unreproving;
But her silence says—what she never will swear—
   And love seeks better loving.

Go, lady, lean to the night-guitar
   And drop a smile to the bringer,
Then smile as sweetly, when he is far,
   At the voice of an in-door singer.
Bask tenderly beneath tender eyes;
   Glance lightly, on their removing;
And join new vows to old perjuries—
   But dare not call it loving.

Unless you can think, when the song is done,
   No other is soft in the rhythm;
Unless you can feel, when left by One,
   That all men else go with him;
Unless you can know, when upraised by his breath,
   That your beauty itself wants proving;
Unless you can swear, " For life, for death !"—
   Oh, fear to call it loving!

Unless you can muse in a crowd all day,
   On the absent face that fixed you;

Unless you can love, as the angels may,
    With the breadth of heaven betwixt you;
Unless you can dream that his faith is fast,
    Through behoving and unbehoving;
Unless you can *die* when the dream is past—
    Oh, never call it loving!

A MAN'S REQUIREMENTS.

Love me, Sweet, with all thou art,
    Feeling, thinking, seeing;
Love me in the lightest part,
    Love me in full being.

Love me with thine open youth
    In its frank surrender;
With the vowing of thy mouth.
    With its silence tender.

Love me with thine azure eyes,
    Made for earnest granting;
Taking color from the skies,
    Can Heaven's truth be wanting?

Love me with their lids, that fall
    Snow-like at first meeting;
Love me with thine heart, that all
    Neighbors then see beating.

A MAN'S REQUIREMENTS.

Love me with thine hand stretched out
   Freely—open-minded:
Love me with thy loitering foot,—
   Hearing one behind it.

Love me with thy voice, that turns
   Sudden faint above me;
Love me with thy blush that burns
   When I murmur, *Love me!*

Love me with thy thinking soul,
   Break it to love-sighing;
Love me with thy thoughts that roll
   On through living—dying.

Love me in thy gorgeous airs,
   When the world has crowned thee;
Love me, kneeling at thy prayers,
   With the angels round thee.

Love me pure, as musers do,
   Up the woodlands shady:
Love me gaily, fast and true,
   As a winsome lady.

Through all hopes that keep us brave,
   Further off or nigher,
Love me for the house and grave,
   And for something higher.

Thus, if thou wilt prove me, Dear,
    Woman's love no fable,
I will love *thee*—half a year—
    As a man is able.

INCLUSIONS.

Oh, wilt thou have my hand, Dear, to lie along in thine?
As a little stone in a running stream, it seems to lie and pine.
Now drop the poor pale hand, Dear, unfit to plight with thine.

Oh, wilt thou have my cheek, Dear, drawn closer to thine own?
My cheek is white, my cheek is worn, by many a tear run down.
Now leave a little space, Dear, lest it should wet thine own.

Oh, must thou have my soul, Dear, commingled with thy soul?—
Red grows the cheek, and warm the hand; the part is in the whole:
Nor hands nor cheeks keep separate, when soul is joined to soul.

LOVE FOR LOVE.

FROM THE PORTUGUESE.

If thou must love me, let it be for nought
Except for love's sake only. Do not say
" I love her for her smile—her look—her way

Of speaking gently,—for a trick of thought
That falls in well with mine, and certes brought
A sense of pleasant ease on such a day"—
For these things in themselves, Belovèd, may
Be changed, or change for thee,—and love, so wrought,
May be unwrought so. Neither love me for
Thine own dear pity's wiping my cheeks dry,—
A creature might forget to weep, who bore
Thy comfort long, and lose thy love thereby!
But love me for love's sake, that evermore
Thou may'st love on, through love's eternity.

A LOCK OF HAIR.

FROM THE PORTUGUESE.

I NEVER gave a lock of hair away
To a man, Dearest, except this to thee,
Which now upon my fingers thoughtfully
I ring out to the full brown length and say
"Take it." My day of youth went yesterday;
My hair no longer bounds to my foot's glee,
Nor plant I it from rose or myrtle-tree,
As girls do, any more: it only may
Now shade on two pale cheeks the mark of tears,
Taught dropping from the head that hangs aside
Through sorrow's trick. I thought the funeral-shears
Would take this first, but Love is justified,—

Take it thou,—finding pure, from all those years,
The kiss my mother left here when she died.

CALL ME BY MY PET-NAME.

FROM THE PORTUGUESE.

Yes, call me by my pet-name! let me hear
The name I used to run at, when a child,
From innocent play, and leave the cowslips piled,
To glance up in some face that proved me dear
With the look of its eyes. I miss the clear
Fond voices which, being drawn and reconciled
Into the music of Heaven's undefiled,
Call me no longer. Silence on the bier,
While I call God—call God!—So let thy mouth
Be heir to those who are now exanimate.
Gather the north flowers to complete the south,
And catch the early love up in the late.
Yes, call me by that name,—and I, in truth,
With the same heart, will answer and not wait.

THE KISS.

FROM THE PORTUGUESE.

First time he kissed me, he but only kissed
The fingers of this hand wherewith I write;

And ever since, it grew more clean and white,
Slow to world-greetings, quick with its "Oh, list,"
When the angels speak. A ring of amethyst
I could not wear here, plainer to my sight,
Than that first kiss. The second passed in height
The first, and sought the forehead, and half missed,
Half falling on the hair. Oh beyond meed!
That was the chrism of love, which love's own crown,
With sanctifying sweetness, did precede.
The third upon my lips was folded down
In perfect, purple state; since when, indeed,
I have been proud and said, " My love, my own."

THE BEST THING IN THE WORLD.

What's the best thing in the world?
June-rose, by May-dew impearled;
Sweet south-wind, that means no rain;
Truth, not cruel to a friend;
Pleasure, not in haste to end;
Beauty, not self-decked and curled
Till its pride is over-plain;
Light, that never makes you wink;
Memory, that gives no pain;
Love, when, *so,* you're loved again.
What's the best thing in the world?
—Something out of it, I think.

THE CRY OF THE HUMAN.

"There is no God," the foolish saith,
    But none, "There is no sorrow,"
And nature oft the cry of faith,
    In bitter need will borrow:
Eyes, which the preacher could not school,
    By wayside graves are raisèd,
And lips say, "God be pitiful,"
    Who ne'er said, "God be praisèd."
               Be pitiful, O God!

The tempest stretches from the steep
    The shadow of its coming,
The beasts grow tame and near us creep,
    As help were in the human;
Yet, while the cloud-wheels roll and grind,
    We spirits tremble under—
The hills have echoes, but we find
    No answer for the thunder.
               Be pitiful, O God!

The battle hurtles on the plains,
    Earth feels new scythes upon her;
We reap our brothers for the wains,
    And call the harvest—honour:
Draw face to face, front line to line,
    One image all inherit,—

Then kill, curse on, by that same sign,
   Clay—clay, and spirit—spirit.
                Be pitiful, O God!

The plague runs festering through the town,
   And never a bell is tolling,
And corpses, jostled 'neath the moon,
   Nod to the dead-cart's rolling:
The young child calleth for the cup,
   The strong man brings it weeping,
The mother from her babe looks up,
   And shrieks away its sleeping.
                Be pitiful, O God!

The plague of gold strikes far and near,
   And deep and strong it enters;
This purple chimar which we wear,
   Makes madder than the centaur's:
Our thoughts grow blank, our words grow strange,
   We cheer the pale gold-diggers,
Each soul is worth so much on 'Change,
   And marked, like sheep, with figures.
                Be pitiful, O God!

The curse of gold upon the land
   The lack of bread enforces;
The rail-cars snort from strand to strand,
   Like more of Death's White horses:
The rich preach "rights" and "future days,"
   And hear no angel scoffing,

The poor die mute, with starving gaze
  On corn-ships in the offing.
        Be pitiful, O God!

We meet together at the feast,
  To private mirth betake us;
We stare down in the winecup, lest
  Some vacant chair should shake us:
We name delight, and pledge it round—
  "It shall be ours to-morrow!"
God's seraphs, do your voices sound
  As sad, in naming sorrow?
        Be pitiful, O God!

We sit together, with the skies,
  The steadfast skies, above us,
We look into each other's eyes,
  "And how long will you love us?"
The eyes grow dim with prophecy,
  The voices, low and breathless,—
"Till death us part!"—O words, to be
  Our *best*, for love the deathless!
        Be pitiful, O God!

We tremble by the harmless bed
  Of one loved and departed:
Our tears drop on the lips that said
  Last night, "Be stronger hearted!"
O God,—to clasp those fingers close,
  And yet to feel so lonely!

To see a light upon such brows,
   Which is the daylight only!
                Be pitiful, O God!

The happy children come to us,
   And look up in our faces;
They ask us—" Was it thus, and thus,
   When we were in their places?"—
We cannot speak;—we see anew
   The hills we used to live in,
And feel our mother's smile press through
   The kisses she is giving.
                Be pitiful, O God!

We pray together at the kirk
   For mercy, mercy solely:
Hands weary with the evil work,
   We lift them to the Holy.
The corpse is calm below our knee,
   Its spirit bright before Thee—
Between them, worse than either, we—
   Without the rest or glory.
                Be pitiful, O God!

We leave the communing of men,
   The murmur of the passions,
And live alone, to live again
   With endless generations:
Are we so brave?—The sea and sky
   In silence lift their mirrors.

And, glassed therein, our spirits high
    Recoil from their own terrors.
              Be pitiful, O God!

We sit on hills our childhood wist,
    Woods, hamlets, streams, beholding:
The sun strikes through the farthest mist
    The city's spire to golden:
The city's golden spire it was,
    When hope and health were strongest,
But now it is the churchyard grass
    We look upon the longest.
              Be pitiful, O God!

And soon all vision waxeth dull;
    Men whisper, "He is dying;"
We cry no more "Be pitiful!"
    We have no strength for crying:
No strength, no need. Then, soul of mine,
    Look up and triumph rather—
Lo, in the depth of God's Divine,
    The Son adjures the Father,
              BE PITIFUL, O GOD!

MY KATE.

SHE was not as pretty as women I know,
And yet all your best made of sunshine and snow

MY KATE.

Drop to shade, melt to nought in the long-trodden ways,
While she's still remembered on warm and cold days—
      My Kate.

Her air had a meaning, her movements a grace;
You turned from the fairest to gaze on her face:
And when you had once seen her forehead and mouth,
You saw as distinctly her soul and her truth—
      My Kate.

Such a blue inner light from her eyelids outbroke,
You looked at her silence and fancied she spoke:
When she did, so peculiar yet soft was the tone,
Though the loudest spoke also, you heard her alone—
      My Kate.

I doubt if she said to you much that could act
As a thought or suggestion: she did not attract
In the sense of the brilliant or wise: I infer
'Twas her thinking of others, made you think of her—
      My Kate.

She never found fault with you, never implied
Your wrong by her right; and yet men at her side
Grew nobler, girls purer, as through the whole town
The children were gladder that pulled at her gown—
      My Kate.

None knelt at her feet confessed lovers in thrall;
They knelt more to God than they used,—that was all:

If you praised her as charming, some asked what you meant,
But the charm of her presence was felt when she went—
: : : My Kate.

The weak and the gentle, the ribald and rude,
She took as she found them, and did them all good;
It always was so with her—see what you have!
She has made the grass greener even here . . with her grave—
: : : My Kate.

My dear one!—when thou wast alive with the rest,
I held thee the sweetest and loved thee the best:
And now thou art dead, shall I not take thy part
As thy smiles used to do for thyself, my sweet Heart—
: : : My Kate?

AMY'S CRUELTY.

Fair Amy of the terraced house,
: Assist me to discover
Why you who would not hurt a mouse
: Can torture so your lover.

You give your coffee to the cat,
: You stroke the dog for coming,
And all your face grows kinder at
: The little brown bee's humming.

But when *he* haunts your door . . the town
: Marks coming and marks going . .

AMY'S CRUELTY.

You seem to have stitched your eyelids down
    To that long piece of sewing!
You never give a look, not you,
    Nor drop him a " Good morning,"
To keep his long day warm and blue.
    So fretted by your scorning.

She shook her head—"The mouse and bee
    For crumb or flower will linger:
The dog is happy at my knee,
    The cat purrs at my finger.

" But *he* . . to *him*, the least thing given
    Means great things at a distance;
He wants my world, my sun, my heaven,
    Soul, body, whole existence.

" They say love gives as well as takes;
    But I'm a simple maiden,—
My mother's first smile when she wakes
    I still have smiled and prayed in.

" I only know my mother's love
    Which gives all and asks nothing;
And this new loving sets the groove
    Too much the way of loathing.

" Unless he gives me all in change,
    I forfeit all things by him:
The risk is terrible and strange—
    I tremble, doubt, . . deny him.

"He's sweetest friend, or hardest foe,
  Best angel, or worst devil;
I either hate or . . love him so,
  I can't be merely civil!

"You trust a woman who puts forth,
  Her blossoms thick as summer's?
You think she dreams what love is worth,
  Who casts it to new-comers?

"Such love's a cowslip-ball to fling,
  A moment's pretty pastime;
I give . . all me, if anything,
  The first time and the last time.

"Dear neighbor of the trellised house,
  A man should murmur never,
Though treated worse than dog and mouse,
  Till doted on for ever!"

GARIBALDI.

He bent his head upon his breast
  Wherein his lion-heart lay sick:—
"Perhaps we are not ill-repaid;
Perhaps this is not a true test;
  Perhaps that was not a foul trick;
  Perhaps none wronged, and none betrayed.

"Perhaps the people's vote which here
    United, there may disunite,
    And both be lawful as they think;
Perhaps a patriot statesman, dear
    For chartering nations, can with right
    Disfranchise those who hold the ink.

"Perhaps men's wisdom is not craft;
    Men's greatness, not a selfish greed;
    Men's justice, not the safer side;
Perhaps even women, when they laughed,
    Wept, thanked us that the land was freed,
    Not wholly (though they kissed us) lied.

"Perhaps no more than this we meant,
    When up at Austria's guns we flew,
    And quenched them with a cry apiece,
Italia!—Yet a dream was sent . .
    The little house my father knew,
    The olives and the palms of Nice."

He paused, and drew his sword out slow,
    Then pored upon the blade intent,
    As if to read some written thing;
While many murmured,—"He will go
    In that despairing sentiment
    And break his sword before the King."

He poring still upon the blade,
    His large lid quivered, something fell,

"Perhaps," he said, "I was not born
With such fine brains to treat and trade,—
 And if a woman knew it well,
 Her falsehood only meant her scorn.

"Yet through Varese's cannon-smoke
 My eye saw clear: men feared this man
 At Como, where this sword could seal
Death's protocol with every stroke:
 And now . . the drop there scarcely can
 Impair the keenness of the steel.

"So man and sword may have their use;
 And if the soil beneath my foot
 In valor's act is forfeited,
I'll strike the harder, take my dues
 Out nobler, and all loss confute
 From ampler heavens above my head.

"My King, King Victor, I am thine!
 So much Nice-dust as what I am
 (To make our Italy) must cleave.
Forgive that." Forward with a sign
 He went.
 You've seen the telegram?
Palermo's taken, we believe.

ONLY A CURL.

Friends of faces unknown and a land
    Unvisited over the sea,
Who tell me how lonely you stand
With a single gold curl in the hand
    Held up to be looked at by me,—

While you ask me to ponder and say
    What a father and mother can do,
With the bright fellow-locks put away
Out of reach, beyond kiss, in the clay
    Where the violets press nearer than you.

Shall I speak like a poet, or run
    Into weak woman's tears for relief?
Oh, children!—I never lost one,—
Yet my arm's round my own little son,
    And Love knows the secret of Grief.

And I feel what it must be and is,
    When God draws a new angel so
Through the house of a man up to His,
With a murmur of music, you miss,
    And a rapture of light, you forego.

How you think, staring on at the door,
    Where the face of your angel flashed in,
That its brightness, familiar before,
Burns off from you ever the more
    For the dark of your sorrow and sin.

"God lent him and takes him," you sigh;
  —Nay, there let me break with your pain:
God's generous in giving, say I,—
And the thing which He gives, I deny
  That He ever can take back again.

He gives what He gives. I appeal
  To all who bear babes—in the hour
When the veil of the body we feel
Rent round us,—while torments reveal
  The motherhood's advent in power,

And the babe cries!—has each of us known
  By apocalypse (God being there
Full in nature) the child is our own,
Life of life, love of love, moan of moan,
  Through all changes, all times, everywhere.

He's ours and for ever. Believe,
  O father!—O mother, look back
To the first love's assurance. To give
Means with God not to tempt or deceive
  With a cup thrust in Benjamin's sack.

He gives what He gives. Be content!
  He resumes nothing given,—be sure!
God lend? Where the usurers lent
In His temple, indignant He went
  And scourged away all those impure.

He lends not; but gives to the end,
  As He loves to the end. If it seem
That He draws back a gift, comprehend
'Tis to add to it rather,—amend,
  And finish it up to your dream,—

Or keep,—as a mother will toys
  Too costly, though given by herself,
Till the room shall be stiller from noise,
And the children more fit for such joys,
  Kept over their heads on the shelf.

So look up, friends! you, who indeed
  Have possessed in your house a sweet piece
Of the Heaven which men strive for, must need
Be more earnest than others are,—speed
  Where they loiter, persist where they cease.

You know how one angel smiles there.
  Then weep not. 'Tis easy for you
To be drawn by a single gold hair
Of that curl, from earth's storm and despair,
  To the safe place above us. Adieu.

MOTHER AND POET.

TURIN, AFTER NEWS FROM GAETA, 1861.

Dead! One of them shot by the sea in the east,
And one of them shot in the west by the sea.

Dead! both my boys! When you sit at the feast
   And are wanting a great song for Italy free,
      Let none look at *me!*

Yet I was a poetess only last year,
   And good at my art, for a woman, men said;
But *this* woman, *this*, who is agonized here,
   —The east sea and west sea rhyme on in her head
      For ever instead.

What art can a woman be good at? Oh, vain!
   What art *is* she good at, but hurting her breast
With the milk-teeth of babes, and a smile at the pain?
   Ah boys, how you hurt! you were strong as you pressed,
      And I proud, by that test.

What art 's for a woman? To hold on her knees
   Both darlings! to feel all their arms round her throat,
Cling, strangle a little! to sew by degrees
   And 'broider the long-clothes and neat little coat;
      To dream and to doat.

To teach them . . It stings there! *I* made them indeed
   Speak plain the word *country.* *I* taught them, no doubt,
That a country 's a thing men should die for at need.
   I prated of liberty, rights, and about
      The tyrant cast out.

And when their eyes flashed . . O my beautiful eyes! . .
   I exulted; nay, let them go forth at the wheels

Of the guns, and denied not. But then the surprise
    When one sits quite alone! Then one weeps, then one kneels!
        God, how the house feels!

At first, happy news came, in gay letters moiled
    With my kisses,—of camp-life and glory, and how
They both loved me; and, soon coming home to be spoiled,
    In return would fan off every fly from my brow
        With their green laurel-bough.

Then was triumph at Turin: "Ancona was free!"
    And some one came out of the cheers in the street,
With a face pale as stone, to say something to me.
    My Guido was dead! I fell down at his feet,
        While they cheered in the street.

I bore it; friends soothed me; my grief looked sublime
    As the ransom of Italy. One boy remained
To be leant on and walked with, recalling the time
    When the first grew immortal, while both of us strained
        To the height he had gained.

And letters still came, shorter, sadder, more strong,
    Writ now but in one hand, "I was not to faint,—
One loved me for two—would be with me ere long:
    And *Viva l' Italia!*—he died for, our saint,
        Who forbids our complaint."

My Nanni would add, "he was safe, and aware
    Of a presence that turned off the balls,—was imprest

It was Guido himself, who knew what I could bear,
   And how 't was impossible, quite dispossessed,
      To live on for the rest."

On which, without pause, up the telegraph-line
   Swept smoothly the next news from Gaeta :—*Shot.*
Tell his mother. Ah, ah, "his," "their" mother,—not "mine,"
   No voice says "*My* mother" again to me. What!
      You think Guido forgot?

Are souls straight so happy that, dizzy with Heaven,
   They drop earth's affections, conceive not of woe?
I think not. Themselves were too lately forgiven
   Through THAT Love and Sorrow which reconciled so
      The Above and Below.

O Christ of the five wounds, who look'dst through the dark
   To the face of Thy mother! consider, I pray,
How we common mothers stand desolate, mark,
   Whose sons, not being Christs, die with eyes turned away,
      And no last word to say!

Both boys dead? but that's out of nature. We all
   Have been patriots, yet each house must always keep one.
'Twere imbecile, hewing out roads to a wall;
   And, when Italy's made, for what end is it done
      If we have not a son?

Ah, ah, ah! when Gaeta's taken, what then?
   When the fair wicked queen sits no more at her sport

Of the fire-balls of death crashing souls out of men?
  When the guns of Cavalli with final retort
    Have cut the game short?

When Venice and Rome keep their new jubilee,
  When your flag takes all heaven for its white, green and red,
When *you* have your country from mountain to sea,
  When King Victor has Italy's crown on his head,
    (And *I* have my Dead)—

What then? Do not mock me. Ah, ring your bells low,
  And burn your lights faintly! *My* country is *there*,
Above the star pricked by the last peak of snow:
  My Italy's THERE, with my brave civic Pair,
    To disfranchise despair!

Forgive me. Some women bear children in strength,
  And bite back the cry of their pain in self-scorn;
But the birth-pangs of nations will wring us at length
  Into wail such as this—and we sit on forlorn
    When the man-child is born.

Dead! One of them shot by the sea in the east,
  And one of them shot in the west by the sea.
Both! both my boys! If in keeping the feast
  You want a great song for your Italy free,
    Let none look at *me*!

[This was Laura Savio, of Turin, a poetess and patriot, whose sons were killed at Ancona and Gaeta.]

NAPOLEON III. IN ITALY.

I.

Emperor, Emperor!
From the centre to the shore,
From the Seine back to the Rhine,
Stood eight millions up and swore
By their manhood's right divine
   So to elect and legislate,
This man should renew the line
Broken in a strain of fate
And leagued kings at Waterloo,
When the people's hands let go.
     Emperor
     Evermore.

II.

With a universal shout
They took the old regalia out
From an open grave that day;
From a grave that would not close,
Where the first Napoleon lay
   Expectant, in repose,
As still as Merlin, with his conquering face
Turned up in its unquenchable appeal
To men and heroes of the advancing race,
   Prepare to set the seal
Of what has been on what shall be.
     Emperor
     Evermore.

III.

The thinkers stood aside
To let the nation act.
Some hated the new-constituted fact
Of empire, as pride treading on their pride.
Some quailed, lest what was poisonous in the past
Should graft itself in that Druidic bough
    On this green now.
  Some cursed, because at last
The open heavens to which they had look'd in vain
For many a golden fall of marvellous rain
  Were closed in brass; and some
Wept on because a gone thing could not come;
And some were silent, doubting all things for
    That popular conviction,—evermore
    Emperor.

IV.

That day I did not hate
Nor doubt, nor quail, nor curse.
I, reverencing the people, did not hate
My reverence of their deed and oracle,
  Nor vainly prate
  Of better and of worse
Against the great conclusion of their will.
  And yet, O voice and verse,
Which God set in me to acclaim and sing
Conviction, exaltation, aspiration,
We gave no music to the patent thing,

Nor spared a holy rhythm to throb and swim
    About the name of him
Translated to the sphere of domination
    By democratic passion!
    I was not used, at least,
    Nor can be, now or then,
    To stroke the ermine beast
    On any kind of throne,
(Though builded by a nation for its own,)
And swell the surging choir for kings of men—
    "Emperor
    Evermore."

v.

    But now, Napoleon, now
That, leaving far behind the purple throng
    Of vulgar monarchs, thou
    Tread'st higher in thy deed
    Than stair of throne can lead
    To help in the hour of wrong
The broken hearts of nations to be strong.—
Now, lifted as thou art
To the level of pure song,
We stand to meet thee on these Alpine snows!
And while the palpitating peaks break out
Ecstatic from somnambular repose
With answers to the presence and the shout,
We, poets of the people, who take part
With elemental justice, natural right,

Join in our echoes also, nor refrain.
We meet thee, O Napoleon, at this height
At last, and find thee great enough to praise.
Receive the poet's chrism, which smells beyond
   The priest's and pass thy ways;—
An English poet warns thee to maintain
God's word, not England's :—let His truth be true
And all men liars! with His truth respond
To all men's lie. Exalt the sword and smite
On that long anvil of the Apennine
Where Austria forged the Italian chain in view
Of seven consenting nations, sparks of fine
   Admonitory light,
Till men's eyes wink before convictions new.
Flash in God's justice to the world's amaze,
Sublime Deliverer!—after many days
Found worthy of the deed thou art come to do—
   Emperor
   Evermore.

VI.

But Italy, my Italy,
Can it last, this gleam?
Can she live and be strong,
Or is it another dream
Like the rest we have dreamed so long?
   And shall it, must it be,
That after the battle-cloud has broken
She will die off again

Like the rain,
Or like a poet's song
Sung of her, sad at the end
Because her name is Italy,—
Die and count no friend?
It is true,—may it be spoken,
That she who has lain so still,
With a wound in her breast,
And a flower in her hand,
And a grave-stone under her head,
While every nation at will
Beside her has dared to stand
And flout her with pity and scorn,
Saying, " She is at rest,
She is fair, she is dead,
And, leaving room in her stead
To Us who are later born,
This is certainly best !"
Saying, " Alas, she is fair,
Very fair, but dead,
And so we have room for the race."
—Can it be true, be true,
That she lives anew?
That she rises up at the shout of her sons
At the trumpet of France,
And lives anew?—is it true
That she has not moved in a trance,
As in Forty-eight?

When her eyes were troubled with blood
Till she knew not friend from foe,
Till her hand was caught in a strait
Of her cerement and baffled so
From doing the deed she would;
And her weak foot stumbled across
The grave of a king,
And down she dropt at heavy loss,
And we gloomingly covered her face and said,
"We have dreamed the thing;
She is not alive, but dead."

VII.

Now, shall we say
Our Italy lives indeed?
And if it were not for the beat and bray
Of drum and trump of martial men,
Should we feel the underground heave and strain,
Where heroes left their dust as a seed
   Sure to emerge one day?
And if it were not for the rhythmic march
Of France and Piedmont's double hosts,
   Should we hear the ghosts
Thrill through ruined aisle and arch,
Throb along the frescoed wall,
Whisper an oath by that divine
They left in picture, book and stone
   That Italy is not dead at all?
Ay, if it were not for the tears in our eyes

These tears of a sudden passionate joy
    Should we see her arise
From the place where the wicked are overthrown,
    Italy, Italy? loosed at length
    From the tyrant's thrall,
Pale and calm in her strength?
Pale as the silver cross of Savoy
When the hand that bears the flag is brave,
And not a breath is stirring, save
    What is blown
Over the war-trump's lip of brass,
Ere Garibaldi forces the pass!

VIII.

    Ay, it is so, even so.
    Ay; and it shall be so.
Each broken stone that long ago
She flung behind her as she went
In discouragement and bewilderment
Through the cairns of Time, and missed her way
    Between to-day and yesterday,
    Up springs a living man.
And each man stands with his face in the light
    Of his own drawn sword,
Ready to do what a hero can.
Wall to sap, or river to ford,
Cannon to front, or foe to pursue,
Still ready to do, and sworn to be true,
    As a man and a patriot can.

Piedmontese, Neapolitan,
Lombard, Tuscan, Romagnole,
Each man's body having a soul,—
Count how many they stand,
All of them sons of the land,
Every live man there
Allied to a dead man below,
And the deadest with blood to spare
To quicken a living hand
In case it should ever be slow.
Count how many they come
To the beat of Piedmont's drum,
With faces keener and grayer
Than swords of the Austrian slayer,
All set against the foe.
 " Emperor
 Evermore."

IX.

Out of the dust, where they ground them,
Out of the holes, where they dogged them,
Out of the hulks, where they wound them
In iron, tortured and flogged them;
Out of the streets, where they chased them,
Taxed them and then bayoneted them,—
Out of the homes, where they spied on them,
(Using their daughters and wives,)
Out of the church, where they fretted them,
Rotted their souls and debased them,

Trained them to answer with knives,
Then cursed them all at their prayers!—
Out of cold lands, not theirs,
Where they exiled them, starved them, lied on them;
Back they come like a wind, in vain
Cramped up in the hills, that roars its road
The stronger into the open plain;
Or like a fire that burns the hotter
And longer for the crust of cinder,
Serving better the ends of the potter;
Or like a restrained word of God,
Fulfilling itself by what seems to hinder.
 " Emperor
 Evermore."

X.

Shout for France and Savoy!
Shout for the helper and doer.
Shout for the good sword's ring,
Shout for the thought still truer.
Shout for the spirits at large
Who passed for the dead this spring,
Whose living glory is surer
Shout for France and Savoy!
Shout for the council and charge!
Shout for the head of Cavour;
And shout for the heart of a King
That's great with a nation's joy.
 Shout for France and Savoy!

XI.

Take up the child, Mac Mahon, though
Thy hand be red
From Magenta's dead.
And riding on, in front of the troop,
   In the dust of the whirlwind of war
Through the gate of the city of Milan, stoop
And take up the child to thy saddle-bow,
Nor fear the touch as soft as a flower
   Of his smile as clear as a star!
Thou hast a right to the child, we say,
Since the women are weeping for joy as those
Who, by the help and from this day,
   Shall be happy mothers indeed.
They are raining flowers from terrace and roof:
   Take up the flower in the child.
While the shout goes up of a nation freed
   And heroically self-reconciled,
Till the snow on that peaked Alp aloof
Starts, as feeling God's finger anew,
And all those cold white marble fires
Of mounting saints on the Duomo-spires
   Flicker against the Blue.
    "Emperor
    Evermore."

   Ay, it is He,
Who rides at the King's right hand!

Leave room to his horse and draw to the side,
Nor press too near in the ecstasy
Of a newly delivered impassioned land:
 He is moved, you see,
 He who has done it all.
They call it a cold stern face;
 But this is Italy
Who rises up to her place!—
For this he fought in his youth,
Of this he dreamed in the past;
The lines of the resolute mouth
Tremble a little at last.
Cry, he has done it all!
 "Emperor
 Evermore."

XIII.

It is not strange that he did it,
Though the deed may seem to strain
To the wonderful, unpermitted,
For such as lead and reign.
But he is strange, this man:
The people's instinct found him
(A wind in the dark that ran
Through a chink where was no door),
And elected him and crowned him
 Emperor
 Evermore.

XIV.

Autocrat? let them scoff,
 Who fail to comprehend
That a ruler incarnate of
 The people, must transcend
All common king-born kings.
These subterranean springs
A sudden outlet winning,
Have special virtues to spend.
The people's blood runs through him,
Dilates from head to foot.
Creates him absolute,
And from this great beginning
Evokes a greater end
To justify and renew him—
 Emperor
 Evermore.

XV.

What! did any maintain
That God or the people (think!)
Could make a marvel in vain?—
Out of the water-jar there,
Draw wine that none could drink?
Is this a man like the rest,
This miracle, made unaware
By a rapture of popular air,
And caught to the place that was best?
You think he could barter and cheat

As vulgar diplomates use,
With the people's heart in his breast?
Prate a lie into shape
Lest truth should cumber the road;
Play at the fast and loose
Till the world is strangled with tape;
Maim the soul's complete
To fit the hole of a toad;
And filch the dogman's meat
To feed the offspring of God?

XVI.

Nay, but he, this wonder,
He cannot palter nor prate,
Though many around him and under,
With intellects trained to the curve,
Distrust him in spirit and nerve
Because his meaning is straight.
Measure him ere he depart
With those who have governed and led;
Larger so much by the heart,
Larger so much by the head.
    Emperor
    Evermore.

XVII.

He holds that, consenting or dissident,
  Nations must move with the time;
Assumes that crime with a precedent
  Doubles the guilt of the crime;

—Denies that a slaver's bond,
   Or a treaty signed by knaves,
(*Quorum magna pars* and beyond
Was one of an honest name)
Gives an inexpugnable claim
To abolishing men into slaves.
      Emperor
      Evermore.

XVIII.

He will not swagger nor boast
   Of his country's meeds, in a tone
Missuiting a great man most
   If such should speak of his own;
Nor will he act, on her side,
   From motives baser, indeed,
Than a man of a noble pride
   Can avow for himself at need;
Never, for lucre or laurels,
   Or custom, though such should be rife,
Adapting the smaller morals
   To measure the larger life.
He, though the merchants persuade,
   And the soldiers are eager for strife,
Finds not his country in quarrels
   Only to find her in trade,—
While still he accords her such honour
   As never to flinch for her sake
Where men put service upon her,

Found heavy to undertake
And scarcely like to be paid:
  Believing a nation may act
  Unselfishly—shiver a lance
(As the least of her sons may, in fact)
  And not for a cause of finance.
    Emperor
    Evermore.

XIX.

Great is he,
Who uses his greatness for all.
His name shall stand perpetually
  As a name to applaud and cherish,
Not only within the civic wall
For the loyal, but also without
  For the generous and free.
  Just is he,
Who is just for the popular due
  As well as the private debt.
The praise of nations ready to perish
  Fall on him,—crown him in view
  Of tyrants caught in the net,
And statesmen dizzy with fear and doubt!
And though, because they are many,
  And he is merely one,
And nations selfish and cruel
Heap up the inquisitor's fuel
To kill the body of high intents,

And burn great deeds from their place,
Till this, the greatest of any,
May seem imperfectly done;
Courage, whoever circumvents!
Courage, courage, whoever is base!
The soul of a high intent, be it known,
Can die no more than any soul
Which God keeps by him under the throne;
And this, at whatever interim,
Shall live, and be consummated
Into the being of deeds made whole.
Courage, courage! happy is he,
Of whom (himself among the dead
And silent), this word shall be said;
—That he might have had the world with him,
But chose to side with suffering men,
And had the world against him when
He came to deliver Italy.
    Emperor
    Evermore.

10

CHRISTMAS GIFTS.

ὡς βασιλει, ὡς θεῳ, ὡς νεκρῳ.
GREGORY NAZIANZEN.

THE Pope on Christmas Day
  Sits in St. Peter's Chair;
But the peoples murmur and say,
  "Our souls are sick and forlorn.
And who will show us where
  Is the stable where Christ was born?"

The star is lost in the dark;
  The manger is lost in the straw;
The Christ cries faintly . . hark! . .
  Through bands that swaddle and strangle—
But the Pope in the chair of awe
  Looks down the great quadrangle.

The magi kneel at his foot,
  Kings of the east and west,
But, instead of the angles, (mute
  Is the "Peace on earth" of their song,)
The peoples, perplexed and opprest,
  Are sighing, "How long, how long?"

And, instead of the kine, bewilder in
  Shadow of aisle and dome,
The bear who tore up the children,
  The fox who burnt up the corn,

And the wolf who suckled at Rome
   Brothers to slay and to scorn.

Cardinals left and right of him,
   Worshippers round and beneath,
The silver trumpets at sight of him
   Thrill with a musical blast:
But the people say through their teeth,
   "Trumpets? we wait for the Last!"

He sits in the place of the Lord,
   And asks for the gifts of the time;
Gold, for the haft of a sword,
   To win back Romagna averse,
Incense, to sweeten a crime,
   And myrrh, to embitter a curse.

Then a king of the west said, "Good!—
   I bring thee the gifts of the time;
Red, for the patriot's blood,
   Green, for the martyr's crown,
White, for the dew and the rime,
   When the morning of God comes down."

—O mystic tricolour bright!
   The Pope's heart quailed like a man's;
The cardinals froze at the sight,
   Bowing their tonsures hoary:
And the eyes in the peacock-fans
   Winked at the alien glory.

But the peoples exclaimed in hope,
"Now blessed be he who has brought
These gifts of the time to the Pope,
When our souls were sick and forlorn.
—And *here* is the star we sought,
To show us where Christ was born !"

A CURSE FOR A NATION.

PROLOGUE.

I HEARD an angel speak last night,
And he said, "Write !
Write a Nation's curse for me,
And send it over the Western Sea."

I faltered, taking up the word :
"Not so, my lord !
If curses must be, choose another
To send thy curse against my brother.

"For I am bound by gratitude,
By love and blood,
To brothers of mine across the sea,
Who stretch out kindly hands to me."

"Therefore," the voice said, "shalt thou write
My curse to-night.
From the summits of love a curse is driven,
As lightning is from the tops of heaven."

"Not so," I answered. "Evermore
    My heart is sore
For my own land's sins: for little feet
Of children bleeding along the street:

"For parked-up honours that gainsay
    The right of way:
For almsgiving through a door that is
Not open enough for two friends to kiss:

"For love of freedom which abates
    Beyond the Straits;
For patriot virtue starved to vice on
Self-praise, self-interest, and suspicion:

"For an oligarchic parliament,
    And bribes well-meant.
What curse to another land assign,
When heavy-souled for the sins of mine?"

"Therefore," the voice said, "shalt thou write
    My curse to-night.
Because thou hast strength to see and hate
A foul thing done *within* thy gate."

"Not so," I answered once again.
    "To curse, choose men.
For I, a woman, have only known
How the heart melts and the tears run down."

"Therefore," the voice said, "shalt thou write
    My curse to-night.

Some women weep and curse, I say,
 (And no one marvels,) night and day.

"And thou shalt take their part to-night,
  Weep and write.
A curse from the depths of womanhood
Is very salt, and bitter, and good."

So thus I wrote, and mourned indeed,
  What all may read.
And thus, as was enjoined on me,
I send it over the Western Sea.

THE CURSE.

BECAUSE ye have broken your own chain
  With the strain
Of brave men climbing a Nation's height,
Yet thence bear down with brand and thong
On souls of others,—for this wrong
  This is the curse. Write.

Because yourselves are standing straight
  In the state
Of Freedom's foremost acolyte,
Yet keep calm footing all the time
On writhing bond-slaves,—for this crime
  This is the curse. Write

Because ye prosper in God's name,
  With a claim
To honour in the old world's sight,

Yet do the fiend's work perfectly
In strangling martyrs,—for this lie
    This is the curse. Write.

Ye shall watch while kings conspire
Round the people's smouldering fire,
  And, warm for your part,
Shall never dare—O shame!
To utter the thought into flame
  Which burns at your heart.
    This is the curse. Write.

Ye shall watch while nations strive
With the bloodhounds, die or survive;
  Drop faint from their jaws,
Or throttle them backward to death.
And only under your breath
  Shall favor the cause.
    This is the curse. Write.

Ye shall watch while strong men draw
The nets of feudal law
  To strangle the weak,
And, counting the sin for a sin,
Your soul shall be sadder within
  Than the word ye shall speak.
    This is the curse. Write.

When good men are praying erect
That Christ may avenge his elect
  And deliver the earth,

The prayer in your ears, said low,
Shall sound like the tramp of a foe
　　That's driving you forth.
　　　　This is the curse.　Write.

When wise men give you their praise,
They shall pause in the heat of the phrase,
　　As if carried too far.
When ye boast your own charters kept true,
Ye shall blush ;—for the thing which ye do
　　Derides what ye are.
　　　　This is the curse.　Write.

When fools cast taunts at your gate,
Your scorn ye shall somewhat abate
　　As ye look o'er the wall,
For your conscience, tradition, and name
Explode with a deadlier blame
　　Than the worst of them all.
　　　　This is the curse.　Write.

Go, wherever ill deeds shall be done,
Go, plant your flag in the sun
　　Beside the ill-doers!
And recoil from clenching the curse
Of God's witnessing Universe
　　With a curse of yours.
　　　　THIS is the curse.　Write.

VOID IN LAW.

Sleep, little babe on my knee,
   Sleep, for the midnight is chill,
And the moon has died out in the tree,
   And the great human world goeth ill.
Sleep, for the wicked agree:
   Sleep, let them do as they will.
Sleep.

Sleep, thou hast drawn from my breast
   The last drop of milk that was good;
And now, in a dream, suck the rest,
   Lest the real should trouble thy blood.
Suck, little lips dispossessed,
   As we kiss in the air whom we would.
Sleep.

O lips of thy father! the same,
   So like! Very deeply they swore
When he gave me his ring and his name,
   To take back, I imagined, no more!
And now is all changed like a game,
   Though the old cards are used as of yore?
Sleep.

"Void in law," said the Courts. Something wrong
   In the forms? Yet, "Till death part us two,
I, James, take thee, Jessie," was strong,
   And ONE witness competent. True

Such a marriage was worth an old song,
   Heard in Heaven though, as plain as the New.
Sleep.

Sleep, little child, his and mine!
   Her throat has the antelope curve,
And her cheek just the color and line
   Which fade not before him nor swerve:
Yet *she* has no child!—the divine
   Seal of right upon loves that deserve.
Sleep.

My child! though the world take her part,
   Saying, "She was the woman to choose,
He had eyes, was a man in his heart,"—
   We twain the decision refuse:
We .. weak as I am, as thou art. . .
   Cling on to him, never to loose.
Sleep.

He thinks that, when done with this place,
   All's ended? he'll new-stamp the ore?
Yes, Cæsar's—but not in our case.
   Let him learn we are waiting before
The grave's mouth, the heaven's gate, God's face,
   With implacable love evermore.
Sleep.

He's ours, though he kissed her but now;
   He's ours, though she kissed in reply;

VOID IN LAW.

He's ours, though himself disavow,
    And God's universe favor the lie;
Ours to claim, ours to clasp, ours below,
    Ours above, . . if we live, if we die.
Sleep.

Ah baby, my baby, too rough
    Is my lullaby? What have I said?
Sleep! When I've wept long enough
    I shall learn to weep softly instead,
And piece with some alien stuff
    My heart to lie smooth for thy head.
Sleep.

Two souls met upon thee, my sweet;
    Two loves led thee, out to the sun:
Alas, pretty hands, pretty feet,
    If the one who remains (only one)
Set her grief at thee, turned in a heat
    To thine enemy,—were it well done?
Sleep.

May He of the manger stand near
    And love thee! An infant He came
To His own who rejected Him here,
    But the Magi brought gifts all the same.
I hurry the cross on my Dear!
    My gifts are the griefs I declaim!
Sleep.

MAY'S LOVE.

You love all, you say,
　Round, beneath, above me :
Find me then some way
　Better than to love me,
Me, too, dearest May!

O world-kissing eyes
　Which the blue heavens melt to!
I, sad, overwise,
　Loathe the sweet looks dealt to
All things—men and flies.

You love all, you say :
　Therefore, Dear, abate me
Just your love, I pray!
　Shut your eyes and hate me—
Only *me*—fair May!

THE FORCED RECRUIT.

Solferino, 1859.

In the ranks of the Austrian you found him,
　He died with his face to you all;
Yet bury him here where around him
　You honor your bravest that fall.

THE FORCED RECRUIT.

Venetian, fair-featured and slender,
   He lies shot to death in his youth,
With a smile on his lips over-tender
   For any mere soldier's dead mouth.

No stranger, and yet not a traitor,
   Though alien the cloth on his breast,
Underneath it how seldom a greater
   Young heart, has a shot sent to rest!

By your enemy tortured and goaded
   To march with them, stand in their file,
His musket (see) never was loaded,
   He facing your guns with that smile!

As orphans yearn on to their mothers,
   He yearned to your patriot bands;—
"Let me die for our Italy, brothers,
   If not in your ranks, by your hands!

"Aim straightly, fire steadily! spare me
   A ball in the body which may
Deliver my heart here, and tear me
   This badge of the Austrian away!"

So thought he, so died he this morning.
   What then? many others have died.
Ay, but easy for men to die scorning
   The death-stroke, who fought side by side.

One tricolor floating above them;
   Struck down 'mid triumphant acclaims

Of an Italy rescued to love them
  And blazon the brass with their names.

But he,—without witness or honor,
  Mixed, shamed in his country's regard,
With the tyrants who march in upon her,
  Died faithful and passive : 'twas hard.

'Twas sublime. In a cruel restriction
  Cut off from the guerdon of sons,
With most filial obedience, conviction,
  His soul kissed the lips of her guns.

That moves you? Nay, grudge not to show it,
  While digging a grave for him here :
The others have died, says your poet,
  Have glory,—let *him* have a tear.

KING VICTOR EMANUEL ENTERING FLORENCE, APRIL, 1860.

KING of us all, we cried to thee, cried to thee,
  Trampled to earth by the beasts impure,
  Dragged by the chariot's which shame as they roll :
The dust of our torment far and wide to thee
  Went up, darkening thy royal soul.
    Be witness, Cavour,
That the King was sad for the people in thrall
    This King of us all!

King, we cried to thee! Strong in replying,
  Thy word and thy sword sprang rapid and sure,

Cleaving our way to a nation's place.
Oh, first soldier of Italy!—crying
   Now grateful, exultant, we look in thy face.
      Be witness, Cavour,
That, freedom's first soldier, the freed should call
    First King of them all!

This is our beautiful Italy's birthday;
   High-thoughted souls, whether many or fewer,
   Bring her the gift, and wish her the good,
While Heaven presents on this sunny earth-day
   The noble king to the land renewed:
      Be witness, Cavour!
Roar, cannon-mouths! Proclaim, install
    The King of us all!

Grave he rides through the Florence gateway,
   Clenching his face into calm, to immure
   His struggling heart till it half disappear;
If he relaxed for a moment, straightway
   He would break out into passionate tears—
      (Be witness, Cavour!)
While rings the cry without interval,
    " Live, King of us all!"

Cry, free peoples! Honour the nation
   By crowning the true man—and none is truer:
   Pisa is here, and Livorno is here,

And thousands of faces, in wild exultation,
   Burn over the windows to feel him near—
      (Be witness, Cavour!)

And thousands of faces, in wild exultation,
   Burn over the windows to feel him near—
     (Be witness, Cavour!)
Burn over from terrace, roof, window and wall,
   On this King of us all.

Grave! A good man's ever the graver
  For bearing a nation's trust secure;
  And *he*, he thinks of the Heart, beside,
Which broke for Italy, failing to save her,
  And pining away by Oporto's tide:
    Be witness, Cavour,
That he thinks of his vow on that royal pall,
   This King of us all.

Flowers, flowers, from the flowery city!
  Such innocent thanks for a deed so pure,
  As, melting away for joy into flowers,
The nation invites him to enter his Pitti
  And evermore reign in this Florence of ours.
    Be witness, Cavour!
He'll stand where the reptiles were used to crawl,
   This King of us all.

Grave, as the manner of noble men is—
  Deeds unfinished will weigh on the doer:
  And, baring his head to those crape-veiled flags,
He bows to the grief of the South and Venice.
  Oh, riddle the last of the yellow to rags.
    And swear by Cavour
That the King shall reign where the tyrants fall,
   True King of us all!

www.ingramcontent.com/pod-product-compliance
Lightning Source LLC
Chambersburg PA
CBHW031346160426
43196CB00007B/746